SCOTNOTES
Number 31

Eric Linklater's
Private Angelo
and
The Dark of Summer

Christopher Nicol

Association for Scottish Literary Studies 2012

Published by
Association for Scottish Literary Studies
Scottish Literature
7 University Gardens
University of Glasgow
Glasgow G12 8QH
www.asls.org.uk

ASLS is a registered charity no. SC006535

First published 2012

Text © Christopher Nicol

All rights reserved. No part of this book may be
reproduced, stored in a retrieval system, or
transmitted in any form or means, electronic,
mechanical, photocopying, recording or otherwise,
without the prior permission of the
Association for Scottish Literary Studies.

A CIP catalogue for this title
is available from the British Library

ISBN 978-1-906841-11-9

The Association for Scottish Literary Studies
acknowledges the support of Creative Scotland
towards the publication of this book.

ALBA | CHRUTHACHAIL

CONTENTS

	Page
1. Eric Linklater and his work	1
2. Private Angelo: Introduction	8
3. Private Angelo: Synopsis	14
4. Private Angelo: Themes	26
• Loyalty in time of war	26
• Occupation and liberation	29
• The several faces of courage	32
5. Private Angelo: Characters	36
• The men	36
• The women	40
6. The Dark of Summer: Introduction	45
7. The Dark of Summer: Synopsis	50
8. The Dark of Summer: Themes	59
• The corrosive power of memory	59
• Betrayal	61
• The transforming power of war	62
9. The Dark of Summer: Characters	66
10. Bibliography	74

SCOTNOTES

Study guides to major Scottish writers and literary texts

Produced by the Education Committee
of the Association for Scottish Literary Studies

Series Editors
Lorna Borrowman Smith
Ronald Renton

Editorial Board
Ronald Renton
(Convener, Education Committee, ASLS)
Jim Alison
Gillin Anderson
Laurence Cavanagh
Professor John Corbett
Dr Emma Dymock
Dr Morna Fleming
Professor Douglas Gifford
John Hodgart
Catrina McGillivray
Dr David Manderson
Dr Christopher Nicol
Lorna Ramsay
Professor Alan Riach
Dr Christine Robinson
Dr Kenneth Simpson
Lorna Borrowman Smith

THE ASSOCIATION FOR SCOTTISH LITERARY STUDIES aims to promote the study, teaching and writing of Scottish literature, and to further the study of the languages of Scotland.

To these ends, the ASLS publishes works of Scottish literature; literary criticism and in-depth reviews of Scottish books in *Scottish Literary Review*; short articles, features and news in *ScotLit*; and scholarly studies of language in *Scottish Language*. It also publishes *New Writing Scotland*, an annual anthology of new poetry, drama and short fiction, in Scots, English and Gaelic. ASLS has also prepared a range of teaching materials covering Scottish language and literature for use in schools.

All the above publications are available as a single 'package', in return for an annual subscription. Enquiries should be sent to:

> ASLS
> Scottish Literature
> 7 University Gardens
> University of Glasgow
> Glasgow G12 8QH
>
> Tel/fax +44 (0)141 330 5309
> e-mail **office@asls.org.uk**
> or visit our website at **www.asls.org.uk**

Page references are given to the Canongate paperback edition of *Private Angelo*, and to both the Canongate (**C**) and Bloomsbury (**B**) editions of *The Dark of Summer*.

Generous assistance in the preparation of this Scotnote has been received from Professor Isobel Murray.

ERIC LINKLATER AND HIS WORK

Eric Linklater (1899–1974) was one of the most prolific writers of his generation. With twenty three novels, three collections of short stories, half a dozen plays, a volume of poems, two children's novels and an impressive list of biographies, essays and histories to his credit, his place in the canon of Scottish literature might be assumed to be an assured one. But although highly popular with the public in the 1930s and the 1940s, Linklater's style of novel began to fall out of fashion as early as the 1950s, at a time when the post-war generation of novelists began to monopolise the attention of literary critics.

But even at the height of his popularity with the novel-reading public, Linklater failed to attract the critical attention he felt he merited. He had little time for the modernist style of writing of poets like T. S. Eliot and novelists such as James Joyce and Virginia Woolf. Unfashionably, he avoided experimenting with streams of consciousness, neologisms, alternative punctuation, invented languages, Freudian ideas and what he calls in Magnus Merriman 'the disruption of language'. Instead, he saw himself primarily as a craftsman, struggling to master language like a traditional Scottish makar, whose chief aim was to narrate his tale with consummate clarity, in a style appropriate to the topic in hand, in language that was to be savoured for its own sake. Writing of his art in his 1941 autobiography, *The Man on My Back*, he comments:

> I have an active imagination, and in a modest way am capable of invention. I have also an interest in words which is like an honest carpenter's interest in wood. Bring together these two conditions, and you have a novelist condemned to work [...] The finding, development and first rough shaping of an idea are among the most compulsive and overwhelming pleasures under the sun. [...] Then comes the finer shaping, the forcing into a pattern, the bending of thought, the discarding of words, the comparing of two good words to find the better. (p. 198)

His philosophy of the novel harked back to that of an earlier era of writing, that of Arnold Bennett, John Galsworthy and E. M. Forster, when telling a story was central to a novelist's aims. In addition, unlike many modernist novelists, Linklater did not share their vision of a society irredeemably fractured and fragmented. Equally unfashionably for a writer of his era, he saw the human condition, while infinitely flawed, as still capable of redemption and what he talks of in *The Dark of Summer* as 'wholeness'. Both novels discussed here believe wholeheartedly in the triumph of the human spirit over destructive forces within and without the characters.

Eric Linklater was born in 1899 in Penarth, South Wales, although he never publicly admitted this until he was over seventy. He was not slow to cultivate the myth that grew up around him that he was, like his father before him, a native of Orkney. For identification with these northern islands had come to forge the essence of his personality both as man and writer.

While his father was employed as master mariner based in Cardiff, Linklater spent his school holidays on his grandfather's croft until his father built a family home nearby. The time spent here saw the young Eric developing a powerful love of these northern landscapes which he revisits evocatively in his prose:

> [...] beneath a changing sky Orkney can change from ugliness and bleakness to a radiant panorama of lakes more brightly blue than the Mediterranean, a dazzling chequer-board of grass and ploughland, the shadow-and-claret of hills that flow in sweet unbroken lines. It can put on beauty like a song or a dance, so light and airy it is, so brisk and tender, and gay. And then, in less time than it takes to count the colours, the colours will change again, and the land looks grave and peaceful. [*Scottish Country* ed. George Scott-Moncrieff (London: Wishart, 1935) From an essay 'Orkney' p.82]

But as well as celebrating Orcadian landscapes, Linklater was drawn to Orkney's Viking dark ages past, a fascination which confirmed Orkney as his spiritual home and found its fullest expression in his 1932 novel *The Men of Ness*, although his love of Norse seafaring legends emerges in other novels and short stories. In 1955 he published *The Ultimate Viking*, a survey of the Viking sagas and an attempt to understand the motivation of the Norsemen and their importance to British history.

When Linklater's father changed employer and became captain of a London registered merchant ship on the Far Eastern routes, the family left Wales and settled in Aberdeen which made for greater ease of travel to and from Orkney. Eric attended Lord Byron's old school, Aberdeen Grammar School, where he distinguished himself academically all round, developing even at that early age that strong relish for the elegantly structured sentence ('the finer shaping') and carefully selected word ('the comparing of two good words to find the better') which is apparent in all his later writing, whatever the genre.

In 1916, the year his father died, Eric enrolled as a medical student at Aberdeen University, largely to please his mother rather than through any personal passion for medicine. But his prime concern at the time was to get into the war which was raging throughout Europe. At the end of his first two terms, at the age of eighteen, he enrolled in the Fife & Forfar Yeomanry and was soon bound for France where, promoted to lance-corporal and transferred to the Black Watch, he was engaged as a sniper.

Here we see one of the paradoxes of Linklater's life emerging. Linklater, the writer who saw the follies of war more clearly than most, loved army life and the camaraderie it brought. His biographer, Michael Parnell, notes:

> It was not the Army itself which was the true object of his affections, but the men who made it up. The Army was a monolithic and imperfect institution which often enough was boring and irritating, inefficient in its use of men, cluttered in its operations by red tape of unimaginable proportions, and irrational in its actions. The men were a different matter: they were bound together by causes and

circumstances, ready to give everything for their countries, families, wives and sweethearts, and sharing in some measure the most heroic and delightful characteristics of mankind at its best: courage, humour and friendship.[1]

In the two novels discussed here, *Private Angelo* and *The Dark of Summer*, we see this unsentimental gaze at the folly and cruelty of war warmed by a compassionate understanding of the motivations and emotions of soldiers as they confront and attempt to survive it.

Severely wounded in the head, he was repatriated and spent the rest of the war in Edinburgh and Fort George. His army career was a formative influence on several novels, and provided much of the source material for the two novels under study here. We also find army life recurring in others such as *Roll of Honour, Position at Noon* and, memorably, in the opening chapter of *Magnus Merriman*. It is also dealt with most fully in his third volume of autobiography *Fanfare for a Tin Hat*. It is perhaps no coincidence that his last work (completed by his son Andro) was a history of his beloved Black Watch.

The war over, Linklater resumed his medical studies at Aberdeen but it became increasingly apparent that his heart was not in it and before long he transferred from Marischal College to King's College to read English Literature under A. A. Jack. He threw himself into the literary, dramatic, political and debating activities of the university with enormous enthusiasm but still managed to emerge with a First Class Honours degree, along with several university prizes.

After graduating, he worked briefly for the Aberdeen *Press and Journal* before landing the job of assistant editor of *The Times of India* in October 1925. The attraction here was the opportunity to travel, for like the Vikings he so much admired, Linklater was an inveterate traveller, a passion that remained with him throughout his life.

While convinced his career would be connected with writing in some way, he was not keen on the life of an office-bound journalist and in April 1927, cutting short a three year contract, began a leisurely return journey to Britain via

Karachi, Baghdad, Teheran, Baku, Batum and Vienna. Once home, he was reluctant to resume full-time journalism but did occasional work for *Blackwood's Magazine* and the *Daily Mail* while he worked on his poetry and verse plays where, initially, he felt he would make his literary mark. A volume of poetry, *A Dragon Laughed*, appeared in 1930 but Linklater was the first to admit his approach to poetry was out of tune with the modern age and he made no further attempt at seriously establishing his literary reputation in this area.

He found employment as a lecturer at Aberdeen University while he pondered his literary future. Inspired by the success of a university contemporary in publishing her first novel, he began work on an idea which had first come to him in India and, in March 1928, *White-Maa's Saga* was completed (and published a year later). This is a novel deals with a young Orcadian who, after service in the army in the First World War, struggles, rather like Linklater himself, with medical studies at Inverdoon, a thinly disguised Aberdeen.

Linklater now applied for a Commonwealth Fellowship with a view to travelling to the United States for two years. He was successful and set off for New York in October 1928 and while in America worked on his second novel, *Poet's Pub*, which was brought out by Jonathan Cape in 1929.

Although based academically in Cornell and later Berkeley, he travelled widely throughout America, soaking up material which was to find expression in his first major publishing success, the satirical novel *Juan in America* which appeared in 1931. By the end of the year it had gone through nine impressions and made Linklater financially independent as a writer. The blockbuster triumph of *Juan* meant that Linklater had found his true literary direction and his prolific writing career was now well under way.

1933 saw Linklater back in Scotland, standing as a candidate in East Fife for the National Party of Scotland, a forerunner of the Scottish National Party. He came fifth in a field of five and, after falling out with the party machine, rather turned his back on politics, although this episode did furnish him with hilarious material for yet another publishing success, *Magnus Merriman*, which appeared the following year.

A rather more successful event in June 1933 was his marriage to Marjorie MacIntyre, his lifelong companion who bore him four children. The newlyweds decided to winter in Italy and set up home first in Lerici before moving to Fiesole where Eric worked on a commission to write a biography of Robert the Bruce. In Fiesole they were the guests of the critic and biographer Percy Lubbock, to whose wife, Lady Sybil, Linklater was indebted for the phrase *dono di coraggio* which remained with him and became central to the depicting of the eponymous hero of his 1946 novel, *Private Angelo*. It was used in the context of a story she recounted about an Italian peasant in the First World War and it was from here the germ of the idea for *Private Angelo* first began to grow, although it would require Linklater's further experiences in wartime Italy to refine and develop it fully.

The outbreak of the Second World War saw the now Orkney-based Linklater busy with the Coastal Defence unit of the Territorial Army. As the war progressed, he became as much occupied with soldiering as with writing. His military efforts saw him rewarded with a promotion to major in November 1939 but he hankered to do more for the war effort. The opportunity came when he was invited to use his writing talents in the service of the War Office in the Directorate of Public Relations to help publicise the government's war work to the public at large. Amongst his many propaganda duties there was one to write a pamphlet detailing the war effort in, among other places, the Faeroes, which furnished him with much information which would be useful in the writing of *The Dark of Summer* more than a decade later. This was a hectic period for Linklater, travelling around Britain collating war effort information but also coping with the writing and recording demands of a broadcasting career which had taken off during the early war years.

In 1944 he was assigned to following the Allied attack on Italy and to documenting events for a history of the campaign which appeared in 1951. In so doing, he gathered material which was to serve him well in delineating not only Tony Chisholm's progress through the Garigliano Valley in

The Dark of Summer but also in portraying the people and places in the world of *Private Angelo*.

Peacetime found Linklater moving from his beloved Orkney to the mainland, largely to accommodate the needs of a growing family, where at Pitcalzean near Nigg in Ross-shire he spent much of the rest of his productive writing life until, driven by the growing industrialisation of Nigg, he moved in 1972 to the Mains of Haddo, not far from Aberdeen where his writing career had begun. He died on the 7th of November 1974 and is buried by the Loch of Harray in Orkney.

Notes
1 Parnell 1984:20

PRIVATE ANGELO: INTRODUCTION

Private Angelo, like *The Dark of Summer*, is a novel about the individual trying to make sense of himself and his situation in war and its aftermath. Angelo is a hapless innocent, lacking the *dono di coraggio* ('gift of courage'), who is buffeted by the ever-changing military situation in an Italy on the brink of liberation. Although lacking in physical courage, Angelo emerges as a likeable character whose clear-sighted comments on the realities of war and liberation stand in sharp contrast to the self-serving 'philosophising' of his amoral father. His moral, rather than physical, courage sees him finding eventual happiness in a radically reshaped post-war world, endorsing Linklater's belief in the ultimate triumph of human decency over the dark forces that threaten it throughout the novel.

Unlike *The Dark of Summer*, however, which was the result of more than a decade of post-war reflection, *Private Angelo* is the issue of the heat of war, being partly written in Rome in 1944 and finished in Orkney in 1945 (with Linklater projecting his cast a few years into an optimistic future). This immediacy of reaction to the catastrophic events of the Second World War was, Linklater always maintained, the reason for its critical neglect. He felt he had

> [...] written of war without apparent bitterness, without manifest anger and open denunciation of its folly; and in the aftermath of war it was obligatory to make one.[1]

While there may be no 'open denunciation', Linklater leaves the reader in little doubt of his hatred of the multiple violations of war and his admiration for the triumph of the human spirit in the face of national and personal devastation. And whatever reservations the critics of the day might have had, the public clearly seemed to share none of them, for the novel sold well on both sides of the Atlantic and was made (although much transformed) into a successful film. When it appeared in 1946, the novel also elicited compliments from members of the Eighth Army and King Umberto of Italy himself. Michael Parnell, Linklater's biographer, finds that it

> [...] embodies the best of all Eric's skills as a writer and all the best qualities of a human being.[2]

But there is more to be said than this, for *Private Angelo* captures much of what might be called the Linklater style, if such a thing may be claimed truly to exist. For Eric Linklater had always prided himself on allowing his subject matter to dictate the tone and voice adopted in his novels. Writing of his early novel *The Men of Ness* in which he attempts to capture the cadences of speech of the characters of the Norse sagas, he commented:

> To a very large extent I have allowed my subjects to determine the style and temper in which I have written of them.[3]

In *The Dark of Summer*, this belief explains the methodical precision we note about the narrative as Tony Chisholm describes in painstaking detail his wartime experiences. We note the insistence on exact dates for many events, which is, of course, exactly what we would expect of the tidy-minded, store-keeping Quartermaster. The narrative style owes much to the rather dry personality of the narrator.

In this approach to writing Linklater felt out-of-step with modernist writers such as D. H. Lawrence and Virginia Woolf who, he felt, imposed their style on every paragraph they wrote. Nevertheless, in many of his most successful works, such as *Juan in America* and here in *Private Angelo*, there are certain characteristics of style that may be detected as recurrent features in Linklater's writing, although categorisation of this most stylistically mercurial of novelists is difficult.

One of these recurrent characteristics is the abrupt juxtaposition of the lightly comic with the gruesomely grotesque: Count Piccologrando, giving a German commander a stern piece of his mind, continues undeterred by the fact that his interlocutor is mortally wounded in a sudden gun salvo; an old cab-horse is left sprawling in cruel distress on the ground after a road accident and while helping calm it, the handsome Angelo finds himself deftly picked up by the gay General Hammerfurter; Angelo is exasperated by an old man falling asleep leaning on him on an overcrowded prison train, but in the morning the old man is found to be dead; Angelo and Lucrezia are engaged in a feisty lovers' quarrel when both are suddenly assaulted and become victims of rape. Linklater's worldview, like that of Shakespeare, embraced the light with the dark:

> I have always thought [...] that the comic attitude to life is just as valid as the tragic attitude. In fact it's probably more valid, because tragedy ends in death and with comedy you have to go on living.[4]

Indeed, it is the commitment to the ongoing business of life in the face of national devastation and personal grief that sustains not only Angelo but all the Italians we encounter here. *Private Angelo*, despite all its tragic happenings, is, in that sense, essentially a comic novel.

Another feature recurrent in Linklater's work is a masterly evocation of place. The Italy of *Private Angelo* is more than an attractive backdrop to the tale: the enduring beauty of the Tuscan landscape as captured by Linklater appears a life force in itself. In a dark moment of reflection as Angelo contemplates the family he has not fathered (yet finds himself responsible for), he is sustained by the Tuscan landscape:

> For I who adore this land of mine, this Tuscany of the green candles and the terraced hills that are crowned with men's houses, adore it because it is complete [...] our olive trees are silver and green, and the olives grow fat. All the countries have come to us, either to conquer or to learn, in love or envy, and we are still Tuscany, and the grapes are ripening again, and in a little while from now, my family [...] will drink the vintage and be the better of it. (p. 241)

Eric Linklater's *Private Angelo* & *The Dark of Summer*

Rome, too, is skilfully recreated in the opening lines:

> In the westering sun the walls of the buildings were the colour of ripe peaches; the domes of several churches rose serenely, firmly round and steeply nippled like the unimpaired and several breasts of a Great Mother [...] Victory in a four-horsed chariot drove superbly through the golden air. Soft green foliage clothed the river-bank, and somewhere a military band was playing a gallant march. How beautiful was Rome, how beautiful all the land of Italy! (p. 1)

Here, this masterly evocation of a Roman evening also captures – in its sensuous references – much of the womanising, self-indulgent, Mussolini-admiring character of the scene's observer, the Count Piccologrando. Landscape painting of this quality is one of Linklater's gifts to literature but it frequently contributes much more than effective poetic description.

Linklater is similarly adept at distilling his own acquired wisdom into witty, often satirical, aphoristic comments placed in the mouths of his characters. The Marchesa Dolce, the Count's comfort-loving mistress, remarks waspishly on the many deprivations brought about by bombings by the Germans and the liberating American and British:

> "If our old friends and our new ones both remain in Italy, we shall soon have nothing left at all." (p. 91)

The pragmatic Lucrezia dismisses talk of courage out of hand:

> "Courage is a common quality in men of little sense," said Lucrezia. "I think you over-rate it. A good understanding is much rarer and more important." (p. 262)

However, often these witty insights are given to Angelo, whose clear-sighted observations of war at first hand see him generalising from his personal experience. Puzzled at hearing guns on the announcement of the armistice, Angelo speculates that they may be British:

> "They may not have heard about it," said Angelo. "The English are frequently unaware of what goes on in Europe." (p. 8)

Invited by the Marchesa Dolce, the Count's mistress, to comment on what war has taught him, Angelo comments:

> "[...] if living at peace were as simple as going to war, we might have more of it." (p. 33)

Meeting columns of refugees on the road fleeing the violence of liberation, Angelo observes to his British friend Simon Telfer:

> "All these people," said Angelo, "have been liberated and now they have nowhere to live. And before the war is over you will have to liberate northern Italy and France, and Greece and Yugoslavia, and Holland and Belgium, and Denmark and Poland and Czechoslovakia."
> "It may take us rather a long time," said Simon.
> "And when you have finished no one in Europe will have anywhere to live." (p. 141)

Commiserating with Annunziata on the displacement of her Polish lover after the Russians annexed his hometown, Lwow, 'because they felt it was their duty', he remarks:

> "We ordinary people always suffer when a great nation develops a sense of duty," said Angelo. (p. 235)

To some, these aphorisms may sound more like the comments of Linklater, the worldly observer, shaking somewhat the stage of his own creation, rather than the spontaneous comments of an Italian peasant lad, but the sheer breadth of Angelo's experiences as he finds himself fighting, observantly, in the Italian, the German and the British armies might well mitigate the charge, for his comments are the distilled wisdom of multiple, painful exposures to human folly in warfare.

Major world events have swept Angelo along causing him mental turmoil and physical distress (including the loss of his left hand), yet there is a lightness of touch here whereby Linklater celebrates not physical courage but the victory of the human spirit and endurance in adversity. Despite his lack of the *dono di coraggio*, Angelo has survived occupation and liberation whose destructive forces have failed to repress his boundless joy in love and beauty. Far from the world of great events, he finds a private peace in his Tuscan farm, rather as Tony Chisholm in *The Dark of Summer* does in far-off Shetland, reflecting on the lessons of war as he confronts the challenges of peace.

Notes
1 Linklater 1970: 316
2 Parnell 1984: 253
3 Linklater 1970: 134
4 Linklater in letter to Mary Marquis 1971.

PRIVATE ANGELO: SYNOPSIS

Chapter One
The novel opens on the eighth September nineteen forty three on the evening when General Eisenhower makes his radio announcement that an armistice had been signed by the Italians and that the war in Italy is over. Listening to the broadcast are Angelo, a handsome young peasant soldier and his 'patron' the Count Agesilas Piccologrando of Pontefiore who is also his commanding officer. Implicit throughout this meeting as the Count mulls nostalgically over the beauties of Angelo's dead mother is the fact that the Count is also in all probability Angelo's father ... Angelo, confessing that he has not the *dono di coraggio* (the gift of courage) and so is a deserter from his unit at Reggio, is roundly rebuked by the Count who speaks proudly of the prowess of the Italian army although he has never actually fought with his regiment, a point that Angelo makes to the Count's discomfort. Despite the proclamation of peace, gunfire is heard and Angelo and the Count go to investigate. They discover that it is the Germans who are firing on whom they consider to be their traitorous allies, the Italians. The Count, remonstrating with them, is about to be arrested by the German when a stray shell fatally wounds the German officer and the Count is temporarily spared imprisonment.

Chapter Two
Having sent flowers to his 'dear friend', the Marchesa Dolce, the Count summons Angelo to tell him that, given the hazards facing Rome as the Germans fight a rearguard action over the city, he is entrusting Angelo with transporting his priceless masterpieces to his estate at Pontefiore for safe-keeping. The Count has made a deal with the German commander von Kluggenschaft whereby in return for the use of two German lorries, he will sell the commander wine at an advantageous price. The pictures are packed up and loaded on the lorries where they are protected by sacks of flour which, it turns out, had been intended for the Italian forces fighting in North Africa but had been 'diverted' by the

Eric Linklater's Private Angelo & The Dark of Summer   15

corrupt Count to save them from being 'wasted' should they be sunk by Allied action. Now they are to be sold for the Count's benefit to the starving peasantry of Pontefiore. Delighted to be returning to his beloved Tuscan village and his boyhood sweetheart, Lucrezia, Angelo mounts the lorry just as the Count is arrested for his part in the previous night's encounter. His crony, von Kluggenschaft, is unable to help him as he has been arrested for consorting with 'a woman of vicious character' (the Count's mistress, the Marchesa Dolce) and the Count is marched off to prison.

Chapter Three
The Czech and Russian lorry drivers (captured prisoners of the Germans) confess their desire to desert and seek and are promised Angelo's help. After his three-year absence, Angelo is warmly welcomed in Pontefiore by the villagers and the Yorkshire-born Countess before setting out to see Lucrezia. Delighting in the sight of Lucrezia (but also of all the other girls of the village as they go about their laundry), Angelo proposes marriage. Dining with Lucrezia's parents he notes 'a fair-haired boy of about twelve months' which he assumes is a new younger brother of Lucrezia or her sister's boy. The pictures are duly secreted along with the Countess' own treasured copies of the complete novels of the author Ouida. The only picture left on display is Angelo's favourite, *The Adoration of the Shepherds*, by Piero della Francesca. Leaving the Countess for Lucrezia, he sees for a second time a fair-haired young man he had noted the day before at the Castle. Rather put out to find Lucrezia deep in conversation with a handsome young man, he repeats, however, his offer of marriage which is rejected by Lucrezia on the grounds that she does not wish to be the widow of a soldier. He returns to Rome with his cargo of wine to be greeted by news of the Count's arrest.

Chapter Four
Angelo and the Marchesa Dolce plot to rescue the Count by offering the wine and a gold watch to the Germans in a complicated barter system. Liberty being impossible for the

moment, the Marchesa arranges for meals to be brought in for her lover (which are promptly consumed by his gaoler) but they are unable to discover the reasons for his arrest. Returning from one such meal delivery, they encounter General Hammerfurter who immediately takes a shine to the handsome Angelo and demands he give him Italian lessons. The Marchesa sees the usefulness of this new contact for pleading the Count's cause. Given the opportunity, Angelo mentions the fact of the Count's wealth which has the desired effect. The greedy German agrees to have him released for five million lire. Angelo is shocked to see the effect prison has had on the Count.

Chapter Five
Although lacking the *dono di coraggio* in war, Angelo shows moral courage in refusing to return to the powerful Hammerfurter as a result of the Germans' treatment of the Count. He now busies himself helping the Czech and the Russian lorry drivers escape by enlisting a friend of a friend called Fest who is much experienced in such matters. Instructed to meet Fest at a trattoria, the two turn up with a mysterious third. The wily Fest fails to turn up, clearly getting wind of the fact this third 'deserter' is a German plant and, when the Germans raid the restaurant, Angelo and the drivers are imprisoned and tortured. Transported to Pesaro to help in the destruction of the town as a defence against the invading Allies, the trio spend time at the beach where Angelo is attracted to the beautiful Annunziata whose husband is also a prisoner. As a means of escape, she suggests that Angelo volunteer for the front line as a means of coming closer to the Allies. Although horrified at being even closer to warfare, Angelo sees the sense of the scheme and reluctantly agrees.

Chapter Six
Back in Rome, the Marchesa and the Count are discussing the nature of government when they are interrupted by a stranger who turns out to be Fest. He has come to tell them while seeking information about the arrest of Angelo, he

discovered that the Count is about to be re-arrested imminently to make money this time for the Gestapo chief. The Count hides under the cushions of the Marchesa's sofa while Fest assumes a military bearing and orders the arresting officers out of the apartment in impeccable German, telling them he is the military attaché to the Vatican. He suggests that they leave Rome temporarily and they set out for a small house the Count owns in Montenero.

Chapter Seven
Ten weeks into serving in the German army, Angelo and his friend Giuseppe, under the influence of stolen brandy, decide to escape. Giuseppe is killed by a landmine which sets Angelo to a miserable reflection on his deserter state since he has now deserted from both the Italian and the German armies and feels responsible for his friend's death since he had been the one to suggest it. His mental torment is cut short by tripping over a root and injuring his knee which sets him to wondering at the beauty of the human body and his spirits rise, particularly when he thinks of his future life with Lucrezia. He decides to make himself known to the Allies and cries out in English. He is immediately answered by a nearby voice. It is that of Major Telfer of the British army who is imprisoned in an upturned jeep. Angelo revives him with his brandy and they are rescued by a British Brencarrier.

Chapter Eight
Telfer is part of a special operations squad where everyone is known by his first name. Angelo is welcomed as Telfer's saviour but is puzzled by the casual appearance of the unit. They explain that their individuality as a unit began in the desert which was an episode they had all relished, a fact which puzzles Angelo even more since he had, to their astonishment, hated his time there in the Italian army. They are as puzzled by Angelo as he is by them. They are interrupted by two rough-looking soldiers carrying a turkey and a goose which they have 'liberated' from the Germans, a term which Angelo disputes but is cut short by the English.

Discussing the matter of 'liberation' with a passing private soldier, Angelo and he take opposite views on the destruction of the village which 'liberation' has brought. While Angelo is saddened, the English soldier, a peacetime bricklayer, is delighted since he knows when he returns home there will be ample employment for him. Needing a driver, Telfer sets off the next morning with Angelo to his base where Angelo learns more about the English, their stoic ways, their politics and their women, all of which leaves him wondering still more about the English and their strange attitudes. On a visit to a neighbouring unit near Monte Cassino, Telfer and Angelo are observing its bombardment by the Allies when they are injured by an ineptly aimed Allied bomb, much to Angelo's irritation with army incompetence. Telfer and Angelo depart for Sorrento.

Chapter Nine
Established in Montenero with the Marchesa, the Count attempts to be philosophic about their reduced circumstances, much to the irritation of his mistress. Out for a walk in the town which is still under German control, the Count is astonished to see Fest reappear and throw a bomb in the direction of a senior Nazi officer and a high-ranking civilian, killing both men. In the following round-up by the Germans, the Count is assaulted and placed under arrest with other citizens of Montenero in a schoolroom. When he regains consciousness, he is told by a fellow prisoner, Toselli, that they are all to be shot. The Count is appalled and reflects on his past life and how little he had pitied the casualties of war before this incident. Ashamed, he says he will go to his death unweeping. Marched to a hillside outside Montenero, the twenty-eight are lined up to be shot when it is announced the assassin has been caught and the prisoners are returned to imprisonment in the town where the Count sees Fest under arrest, his head held high.

Chapter Ten
Telfer's recuperation at Sorrento is cut short when he is recalled to his unit, now at Benevento, for preparation for

Eric Linklater's Private Angelo & The Dark of Summer 19

the final drive to free Italy from the Germans. Telfer is sent on a special mission to break through enemy lines and enter Rome. Angelo is horrified when asked to accompany him and promptly faints. Fearful of losing Telfer's friendship, Angelo finally agrees to go. The special mission entails stopping the Germans blowing up the bridges in Rome across the Tiber. On the way to Rome they are involved in a skirmish which terrifies Angelo further, but pressing on they meet up with a herd of 'the great white cattle of the Tiber' being driven by retreating Germans. Panicking at being so close to the enemy, Angelo leaps from the jeep and accidentally lands on the back of the lead ox which stampedes the others. Angelo is carried off, arriving in a farmyard where he encounters Sergeant Vespucci whom he had last seen when he deserted from his Italian army unit at Reggio.

Chapter Eleven
Vespucci has done well out of the war, having become what he calls 'a Free Distributer' on the black market. News comes of the liberation of Rome and Vespucci and Angelo make their way there where Angelo encounters the Count. (Vespucci at this point, not surprisingly, disappears, having no desire to see the man who is still technically his commanding officer.) The Count is much changed, his hair having turned white although he is reluctant to admit it, his vanity allowing him to confess only to a little grey. He recounts the Montenero episode, adding that Fest along with the other prisoners had escaped as a result of an Allied bombing raid. Saved by a friendly baker's wife and her sister, the Count discovers that, to save face, the Germans had declared all their lost prisoners dead and the Count's goods had been confiscated by the Germans as a result. The Count now accepts fairly philosophically that he has become 'a homeless pauper'.

Chapter Twelve
The Count and Angelo are put up in the Count's old home – denuded of all its goods – by Lorenzo, the butler, and his wife. In the happy throng outside the Vatican Angelo sees in the distance Telfer enjoying the victory celebrations. Angelo

misses Lucrezia at this happy moment but admits to being attracted to a girl in the crowd. The Count is rather more drawn to the Americans whom he sees as generous (despite first hand evidence to the contrary) than to the phlegmatic British. Telfer and Angelo are reunited. Hospitably, Telfer invites the Count to lunch but the Count refuses, preferring to go off enjoy the company of his 'generous' Americans.

Telfer and Angelo leave Rome with Angelo commenting ruefully on the damage that 'liberation' by the Allies has brought Italy. Telfer crisply replies that this was the price of entering the war wilfully and being decisively beaten.

Chapter Thirteen
Advised of her husband's 'death', the Yorkshire-born Countess had borne the news stoically and continued to look after Pontefiore and its inhabitants, sending the young men and girls up into the hills to protect them from the retreating Germans. She also prepares to say farewell to the young, fair-haired man whom Angelo had spotted earlier. He is Tom Trivet, her unhappily married nephew, who had escaped from a prisoner-of-war camp in Libya and made his way to Italy and his aunt's village. There he had had various affairs with the girls, much to his aunt's disapproval, and had organised a group of partisans, word of which had reached the British, leading to him being ordered to join a certain Captain Telfer.

Alone in the castle, the Countess is surprised to see three retreating Germans climbing into the grounds. Led by Captain Schlemmer, they are there to blow up the Pontefiore bridge and prepare defensive positions against the advancing Allies. Boorishly, they demand lodgings and humiliate the Countess. Schlemmer is not without appreciation of art but in the petulance of defeat refuses to respect it, destroying both a pair of priceless Etruscan vases and *The Adoration of the Shepherds* which he cannot bring himself truly to believe is genuine because he feels he is being duped by the Countess, although he is capable of acknowledging its beauty. There is even an indirect invitation to his men to destroy the village itself. Before leaving, his assistant Hoffmeister destroys the

Countess' cherished copies of the works of Ouida in a final act of vandalism at the castle before they set about burning the villagers' valued possessions in the piazza.

Chapter Fourteen

Lucrezia and her sister, Lucia, have been sent by the Countess to help a neighbouring aristocrat overburdened by war refugees. They quarrel and Lucia sets off to see a friend in a nearby village. As the sounds of warfare rage in the distance, Lucrezia falls asleep only to be woken by Angelo who, encountering Tom Trivet and his partisans, has learnt of her presence here. Angelo comments on the likeability of Tom but Lucrezia is reticent in agreeing, finding him, she says, 'shallow and deceitful'. Angelo is anxious that they should marry as soon as possible. Their reunion is interrupted when Lucrezia spots two Goums, Moroccan soldiers with a fearful reputation among women. Fearing for Lucia, she orders Angelo to go and warn her. Angelo is afraid and refuses; she taunts him with his cowardice. Seizing his gun, she sets off to rescue Lucia with Angelo nevertheless accompanying her, pleading with her to think of her own safety. Seeing a Goum suddenly appear nearby, Lucrezia faints and Angelo is knocked unconscious. Awakening, he finds Lucrezia gagged and bound and clearly, like himself, the victim of rape by the Goum. Distraught, she fears Angelo will never marry her now but Angelo replies that they have both been humiliated and that nothing is to be gained by 'mourning for misfortunes that come to us through no fault of our own'. He wants them to put the past behind them and be thankful they are still alive.

Chapter Fifteen

Lucrezia's one thought is now to return to Pontefiore. As they approach the village they see it being bombed – accidentally – by Allied bombers. In the aftermath of the destruction, Lucrezia races off, screaming 'Tommaso'; Angelo heads for the castle and *The Adoration of the Shepherds*. Despite the destruction of much of the painting, he is relieved to find the head of the Madonna intact, which has, with Lucrezia, 'shared his thoughts and his fidelity – the one ideal and the real – in the happiest division'. He finds the Countess somewhat drunk, having taken to drink after the destruction of her prized Ouidas, but who sobers up quickly on hearing of the plight of the village and organises rescue work. Meanwhile, Angelo finds Lucrezia doting over the two year old Tommaso as he plays unconcerned by a pond. Angelo is aghast when it emerges that Tom Trivet is the father and accuses her of betrayal. Philosophically, she retorts that he had been away for three years and she felt sorry for Trivet so far from home. Angelo is scornful of her claim that women may behave in this way in time of war out of charity, but when Tommaso tumbles into the pond for a second time, it is Angelo who rescues him and dries him off.

Chapter Sixteen
This chapter finds Angelo waiting to play his part with Telfer and Trivet in ambush on two senior German officers whom Telfer wishes captured alive. As he waits, Angelo is torn by anguish as he thinks of Lucrezia: at one moment he is violently out of love with her and then memory of her beauty forces him to acknowledge that he does in fact love her. So busy is he in the torment of his thoughts that he fails to play his part properly in the ambush and Telfer's plan is overtaken by Fest now turning up and shooting dead the two Germans, much to Telfer's irritation. A passing German patrol arrives and the partisans scatter with Angelo taking refuge under the dead men's car, on the other side of the road from his comrades. Trivet risks his life by crossing the road under enemy fire to rescue Angelo and is wounded in the process. As they struggle to reach safety Trivet's condition deteriorates seriously and Angelo abandons any lingering resentment towards him as he now knows he owes his life to him. His mind is now made up: he will marry Lucrezia as soon as possible.

Chapter Seventeen
Carrying Trivet to medical help, they encounter the armoured tanks of allied troops who assume care of Trivet while the

others return to Pontefiore where Angelo proposes marriage to a Lucrezia who has lost her scruples about marrying a soldier in time of war and seems totally unconcerned about Trivet's plight. Fest becomes the Countess's guest at the castle. Angelo's joy is diminished when Telfer tells him he has scheduled him for army training and that the war is far from over. The wedding is about to take place in the ruins of the church when Tommaso runs away and falls into a pond again. He can only be comforted by Angelo who gamely goes through the wedding ceremony with a dripping Tommaso sitting on his shoulder. The Countess's unhappiness about being unable to provide an appropriate wedding-feast is abruptly dispelled when a lorry is heard approaching. To the general joy, it is discovered to be the Count himself, accompanied by two American soldiers and ensconced in a lorry filled with supplies of all kinds.

Chapter Eighteen
Relaxing in the castle after the wedding, the Count begins to explain his return with the lorry and the 'Americans'. They are in fact deserters from his old regiment, the older one being Sergeant Vespucci. The latter in his capacity as a Free Distributer had been stealing supplies from a friend of the Marchesa Dolce's, an American colonel, (who himself had been 'exchanging' supplies for Italian art treasures) and keeping them and a stolen lorry in the courtyard of the Count's house. The Count now had a 'dilemma': inform the authorities or insist Vespucci transport the goods to Pontefiore to help the starving villagers. Using his authority as his commanding officer, the Count persuades Vespucci to part with his stolen goods in this way. Fest now announces his intention of travelling to Florence and Bologna to continue his 'hobby' of killing Germans and cannot be convinced to remain with Telfer. He insists on waging war on the Germans in his own individual way. Telfer informs the company that Fest is in fact a German himself who had suffered torture under the Fascists before the war and cannot be persuaded that collective action will right his personal wrongs. He disappears as mysteriously as he had appeared.

Chapter Nineteen

Telfer has proved correct and the war has dragged on. Angelo, after training, is functioning quite well as a soldier in the Cremona Brigade of the Italian army and is quite astonished at his ability to kill in the course of battle. He has not quite become courageous, he admits, but thanks to disciplined training he 'often did not feel afraid for several hours at a stretch'. Much on his mind as he goes into a skirmish is Lucrezia who is about to give birth. In the heat of battle his left hand is injured and has eventually to be amputated. Recuperating, he runs into Annunziata again who is now begging for food to feed her and her months-old child, the son of a Polish soldier whom she had taken up with after the death of her husband at German hands. She has suffered much at the hands of Fascists-turned-Communists for her affair with a foreigner but Angelo, making sure that it is he rather than she who is sorry for the other (a matter of principle to him after what had happened between Lucrezia and Trivet) he decides to look after her and the baby and announces that he will take her back home with him since she has no other means of support, remarking that 'another baby or two will make very little difference in the house'.

Chapter Twenty

On returning home, Angelo is horrified to see the baby Lucrezia has given birth to, the child of the Goum rapist, is black. Lucrezia has little patience with his reaction, pointing out that in war life does not turn out as we would like it to and that they are both lucky to be alive. If he is unhappy with the colour of the baby, she is equally unhappy with the presence of Annunziata. Angelo indulges in a little self-pity, lamenting the fact that as he settles down as a married man he already has three children: a little Englishman, a Pole and a Moroccan. But, unlike before, he has no intention of running from situations he does not like. Indeed, he now sees a certain balance in his situation in that he himself had served in three armies: the Italian, the German and the British 'without wishing to serve in any and now I have three children, none of which I desired'.

His momentary depression is relieved as he looks around him at the beauty and ripeness of the Tuscan landscape, believing that his heterogeneous children can only benefit from its glories. In a quiet way he feels his odd situation has given him a mission: to bring up these children in a way in which destructive obsession with nationality will play no part. Returning home in this spirit of acceptance, Angelo reconciles himself to what has happened between Trivet and Lucrezia and finally Lucrezia accepts what has passed between Annunziata and her husband. When the Count returns in due course, Angelo tells him both Lucrezia and Annunziata are expecting babies. The Count, (assimilating around him, like Angelo, different cultures) arrives home (over the newly reconstructed village bridge) in a German Volkswagen to tell the astonished villagers he has the local agency for an American sewing-machine company.

Chapter Twenty-one
Drink seems to have mellowed the Countess and she becomes thoroughly popular with the villagers in a way that she never had been before; the Count, too, seems a changed figure, less prosperous than before but happier to spend more time in Pontefiore than Rome, whose charms – and those of the Marchesa Dolce – have paled somewhat, as he confides to Angelo. Helped by a young man from Udine, a refugee from ongoing warfare in the Balkans (whose presence reminds us that peace is still by no means universal), Angelo is thoroughly content in his life as a young farmer. Half asleep one afternoon, he hears English voices admiring the courage of the Italians in piecing together their country after the ravages of war. He is delighted to meet again Telfer who, with a friend, is looking up old acquaintances, and even more happy to hear him say that in what he has achieved with his family and farm Angelo has truly the *dono di coraggio* whose lack Angelo had always so bitterly regretted. Lucrezia is less impressed by this accolade, preferring the gift of understanding. But more important than either of these accomplishments, Angelo suggests, is the ability to survive which has brought them through their myriad wartime adventures.

PRIVATE ANGELO: THEMES

Loyalty in time of war
In the course of the novel Angelo serves in the armies of Italy, Germany and Britain; the Count Piccologrando moves his allegiance smoothly from Mussolini to the Americans; Lucrezia's affections fluctuate between Angelo, Tom Trivet and Angelo, while Annunziata is emotionally involved with her husband, Angelo, Stanislas and then Angelo again.

Conventionally, novelists employ loyalty or disloyalty to an individual or a cause as a defining personality trait of their characters. As readers, we are usually invited to applaud the loyal and condemn the disloyal. Clearly, such reactions here are inadequate, for, in varying degrees, these are characters who engage our sympathies despite their sometimes bewildering swings of adherence.

This disruption to our customary responses helps underline in novelistic terms the enormity of the dislocation in the lives of the actual persons concerned. As readers, we are invited to come to terms with unfamiliar reactions just as the citizens of Pontefiore had to come to terms with the unpredictability of destructive events surrounding them. As Lucrezia bitterly comments:

> [...] during the war there were very few of us who had the chance to order our lives as we would have liked them to be. We were little better than sheep, and it was only by good fortune that we escaped the butcher. (p. 239)

Angelo is under no illusions as to the reasons for his service in no less than three armies in one war. He honestly and clear-sightedly admits to lacking the *dono di coraggio* which accounts for his various flights from battlefronts in the Italian (p. 3), the German (p. 66) and the British (p. 119) armies when the violence and horror of the war machine simply became unbearable to him. He has a terror and loathing of all military action and it is chiefly the complicated circumstances of war and liberation rather than any commitment to one side or another which see him taking part in military service in the first place. His fundamental loyalty is to survival and to all that is life-affirming: love (Lucrezia and Annunziata), nature (the land of Tuscany) and creativity (*The Adoration of the Shepherds*).

The Count is less honest than his son in explaining openly the reasons for his changing allegiances, but it quickly becomes clear to readers that the Count's only lasting loyalty is to his own comfort and material advantage. This, however, is frequently disguised under somewhat hypocritical 'philosophising' to justify his doubtful business dealings. For someone who 'prided himself on loyalty' (p. 3) his distancing of himself from his 'friend' Mussolini is accomplished with astonishing speed on the arrival of the Americans. In between times, he had come to a useful commercial arrangement with the Germans in the transport of flour (purloined from the Italian army) to sell to his starving villagers. Admittedly, his relations with the Germans backfire and the Count is seriously impoverished by German actions as unprincipled as his own. His change of loyalty after the armistice is far from ideological, rather a chance to tap into the business opportunities offered by the wealth of the Americans, aided by his own corrupt Sergeant Vespucci who is the Count's lucrative link to the black market. (pp. 218–19) Like Angelo, the Count's loyalty owes little to any ideology and more to survival but, unlike Angelo, he sees survival in materialistic terms.

For the women of the novel, the challenges of loyalty are somewhat different. It is not their loyalty to any cause that is put to the test here, but rather their fidelity to the men in their lives. When compelled by Angelo to confess to the paternity of Tommaso, Lucrezia honestly admits to her affair with Tom Trivet but adds with clear-sighted sadness:

"I have betrayed the man whom I love." (p. 185)

Indeed, when we examine her comments to Lucia (pp. 163–64) there can be no doubting that Angelo is that man nor can we doubt the underlying strength of her love for him, but the circumstances of war have placed cruel strains on her affections. For Angelo had been absent for three years and during that time she had no way of knowing if he were alive or dead. In addition, as she comments to Lucia when the two sisters are lamenting on the absence of their loved ones:

> "It is worse for me," said Lucrezia, "because my nature is more affectionate than yours." (p. 163)

And her lightly flirtatious behaviour with Roberto Carpaccio (p. 28), observed by the returning Angelo would appear to confirm this. While admitting Lucrezia's weakness for handsome men, we should not undervalue her genuine goodness of heart as much as her honesty. As she points out to a fiercely critical Angelo:

> "[...] I was sorry for Trivet in his loneliness, [...]" (p. 187)

Her comments about Angelo to Lucia, however, are sufficient to convince us that this affair was merely a temporary fall from grace, one occasioned by the chaotic circumstances of war, and that her devotion to Angelo remains unimpaired.

Annnunziata's experiences of war reflect a rather similar dilemma: she, too, has to cope with a loved one disappearing in the chaos of war, indeed not once but twice. She, however, has the good fortune finally to encounter an Angelo rather than a Trivet, someone who will sustain rather than abandon her in her need.

Allan Massie, speaking of Linklater's deep understanding of human behaviour, notes that in time of war 'men and women continually do what they could never have imagined themselves doing.'[1] The extraordinary circumstances of war here portrayed – which these characters endure and which they certainly could never have imagined – demand extraordinary reactions from them which cannot be judged by conventional peacetime morality. And they rise to the challenge, each in his or her own way, winning the approbation of even the visiting self-confessed Conservative, Telfer. (p. 259)

The Angelo household which Telfer finds is indeed a far from conventional one: in addition to the three adults, there are the three children of Lucrezia and Annunziata (none of which Angelo had fathered), the baby of Lucrezia and Angelo – and both women are again pregnant. In its happy fertility, it is a household which celebrates, like the novel itself, an all-encompassing loyalty to tolerance, generosity and the human instinct for survival in the face of a brutalising war machine.

Occupation and liberation
Nowhere is Linklater's unshakeable belief in the triumph of the human spirit over the forces of destructive evil more apparent than in *Private Angelo*. Despite the pain and destruction it graphically describes, it is essentially a comic novel. The witty insights of Angelo, the feisty common sense of Lucrezia and the pompous 'philosophising' of the Count raise frequent smiles among readers and Linklater finally leaves Angelo and his extended family in the happy glow of a prospering, fertile Tuscany. Along the way we have been invited to laugh outright at some of the novel's more comic scenes: the Count hiding under the cushions of the Marchesa's sofa, Angelo carried off on the back of a runaway ox or singing opera (badly) to keep Telfer awake in his crashed jeep. Explaining the prevalence of the comic here, Linklater comments in *Fanfare for a Tin Hat*:

> War, in Italy, was a drunken, destructive and impertinent clown; to deal justly and truthfully with it one had to keep one's temper cool, one's judgement clear, and write a comedy. (p. 316)

The ultimate ascendancy of decency and generosity should not blind us, however, to the violent horrors which form the backdrop of this comedy and which Linklater in no way downplays. Indeed, at the novel's heart is the ultimate violation: rape, not only at individual but national level. For the rape of Lucrezia and Angelo by a Goum, part of the liberating French army, personalises and symbolises the wartime atrocities perpetrated against a defenceless population. The forceful attempt by opposing forces to take and hold a helpless Italy leads to painful scenes of utter desolation, witnessed by Telfer and Angelo en route to Rome:

> The pleasant little towns along the Appian way had suffered, quite suddenly, such a change in their appearance as could only have been effected – without the help of science – by long eras of disaster. Our age of steel and explosives had shown itself very like the Ice Age in its ability to alter the face of a landscape, create lacunae, and remove excrescences. Wedding-chamber and warm kitchen, the smithy and the grocer's shop and the notary's office had been reduced to rags and dusty rubble by a stick of bombs that caught the sunlight as they fell. (p. 140)

Press-ganged into helping the Germans in their wanton destruction of the town of Pesaro, Angelo witnesses the human cost of these vicious assaults:

> Most of the houses were quite new, and well-built. The furniture remained in some of them, and when the Germans had taken all they needed for themselves, such as beds and cooking-pots and blankets, they sold what was left to the people who had been evicted. These unhappy creatures used to come every day to watch their houses being demolished, and some of the women cried aloud when they saw the walls tumble. (p. 50)

The far-flung destructive onslaught continues in the taking of Monte Cassino:

> From the mountains beyond Cassino to the lighted water of Gaeta's gulf a thunderstorm of gunfire bellowed among the hills and over the sea and filled the dark valleys with reverberant echoes. An army mustered from the five continents of the world advanced to the attack, to destroy the opposing army of Germany and its subject peoples [...] (p. 108)

Angelo frequently returns to the point that the human cost of liberation by the Allies is as painful as the damage wrought by the Germans:

> "All these people," said Angelo, "have been liberated and

now they have nowhere to live [...] when you have finished no one in Europe will have anywhere to live." (p. 141)

The point is brought nearer home with the nigh total destruction of Pontefiore by Allied bombers:

It was unfortunate that the pilots' information was not up to date. They knew the Germans had occupied Pontefiore, but no one had told them that the Germans had left it. Their bombs, that fell with great accuracy on the chosen targets, were in fact wasted; and so indeed was Pontefiore. (p. 176)

But it is the reaction of both the individual and the population to violation of all kinds by 'liberators' which Linklater is keen to leave us with. Lucrezia, distraught and despairing in the wake of the rape by the Goum, bemoans her fate:

But presently, without raising her head, she spoke to him. "And now," she said, "you will never marry me [...] You will not want to marry me now. You could not, Angelo [...]" (p. 171)

But Angelo responds with a wisdom drawn from the suffering he has encountered:

[...] there is nothing to be gained by going into mourning for misfortunes that come to us through no fault of our own [...] No, Lucrezia, we are not to blame, so the best we can do is to let bygones be bygones, and thank God we are still alive." (p. 171)

This great-hearted acceptance of the ultimate violation is in Linklater's philosophy the only realistic one available to Angelo, Lucrezia and, indeed, the population of Pontefiore if they are to retrieve their lives and build a future for themselves.

Contrasting with Angelo's forgiving attitude in post-liberation life is that of Fest. Fest, whose life we learn from Telfer has been similarly blighted by inhuman treatment at the hands of his fellow Germans, actively continues his bitter campaign against his enemy – but this leads only to his own death.

In this novel, the ultimate liberation would seem to be not from violence but from the bitterness engendered by violence. This, along with the importance of survival, is a lesson which a joyful Angelo, in the novel's closing lines, has clearly drawn from the twin afflictions of occupation and liberation:

> "We have stood up to a great deal, we can stand what is still to come, whether it's poverty or plenty. For we have learnt the most useful of all accomplishments, which is to survive!" (p. 262)

The several faces of courage

Plaguing Angelo for most of the novel is his belief that he lacks the *dono di coraggio*, a state of affairs of which he is acutely ashamed. He sees courage as 'a great and splendid gift' (p. 1) and he spends much of the action berating his cowardice and fear. It is this lack of physical courage that sees him fleeing service in three armies. Of his service in the German army we learn:

> For ten weeks he had served it, and for much of that time his body had felt like a scoured egg-shell. There was no substance in it. Fear had emptied it with a spoon whenever a shell burst near him [...] (p. 66)

He refers frequently to his cowardice. Talking to the Countess he comments:

> "[...] I shall never be a good soldier [...] Because, of course, I have not the *dono di coraggio*." (p. 22)

Suspicious of Annunziata's advice to volunteer for the German front line the more easily to approach the Allies, he sighs:

> "Ah, if only I had the *dono di coraggio!*" (p. 54)

When Simon proposes that Angelo accompany him on his mission behind enemy lines to Rome, Angelo 'fell to the ground in a dead faint'. (p. 109)

Yet we must not overlook the fact that, although he may often be in a state of acute fear, his loyalty to his new-found friends sees him taking part in a planned ambush in the pinewoods of Vallombrosa. But his underlying timidity sees him fleeing under a car when matters go wrong, from where he is rescued by Tom Trivet who is wounded in the process. Moved by Trivet's act of generosity, he feels obliged to match his act of generosity with another. Then Angelo, who throughout the novel has cringed at any mention of battle-front danger, is now somewhat astonishingly heard saying:

"Corporal Trivet needs medical attention, and though it may be difficult to carry him through the German lines, I do not think we should be deterred by that." (p. 201)

But if his strong sense of obligation helps him overcome his physical fear in this instance, we have earlier received glimpses of underlying examples of moral courage which he himself does not appear to notice. Outraged by what he sees as General Hammerfurter's rapacious treatment of the Count he refuses 'with heroic stubbornness' (p. 45) to have any more to do with the powerful commandant of Rome. Towards the end of the novel, we see more and more of this courage to stand up for what he believes to be right: he braves Lucrezia's wrath by insisting that the destitute Annunziata and her child be given a home with them, just as he magnanimously accepts the child of the Goum as his own, as indeed he does with the child which Lucrezia has had with Trivet.

There is, too, a similar kind of moral fortitude abroad in post-war Pontefiore, as the visiting Telfer notes several times:

"When you think the state their country was in, and look at it now [...] you've got to give them credit. Credit for courage as well as hard work. It looked such a hopeless task. Here in Pontefiore, for example [...] Quite hopeless. But they tackled it and they did it. They've got courage [...] They've got something. It's their own sort of courage, but they've got it." (pp. 258–59)

And Telfer, once Angelo had 'explained the ancestry of his family' (p. 260), is quick to acknowledge that he, too, has acquired his own version of that formerly elusive quality:

> "Angelo," said Simon, raising his glass, "have no doubt about it. You possess the *dono di coraggio*." (p. 260)

Angelo's lack of courage may be a burden to him, but the novel explores examples of 'courage' which prove equally problematic. The Count (who throughout the war has led his regiment from the safety of Rome) decides at one point to confront boldly the German authorities when they continue firing on the city after the declaration of the Armistice. This untypical act is more an example of foolhardiness than one of courage, since it results in imprisonment, the loss of a great part of his fortune, the impounding of his home and exile from his beloved Rome.

Fest is someone who is not lacking in courage of his own kind as he wages a one-man war against the Germans. But in indulging his hobby of annoying the Germans, he puts many others at risk: his bold bomb attack in Montenero on two high-ranking Tedeschi leads to arrest of some thirty civilians who are rescued from the firing squad only when Fest is temporarily arrested. He later causes further havoc when, in his desire to take his own personal revenge on the Germans whom Telfer is targeting in the pinewoods of Vallombrosa, he sabotages the planned attack, much to the Englishman's fury:

> Simon, still angry, demanded, "Why did you interfere in this affair? I can't understand you. It seems to me you have shown a complete lack of responsibility."
> "I am self-indulgent," said Fest. "I have nothing in the world but my hobbies." (p. 195)

His 'hobby' has landed Telfer with dead bodies rather than living prisoners, whom he urgently needed for information purposes; it has also led to the wounding of Trivet which has placed the unit in even greater danger as they seek medical help. Such self-regarding action demeans substantially the term 'courage' and is seen by Telfer as 'fundamentally selfish'. (p. 199) It is also self-destructive, as Fest's single-minded, unforgiving response to his fellow Germans ultimately brings about his own death. We can therefore agree with Lucrezia when, despite Angelo's disagreement, she concludes:

"Courage is a common quality in men of little sense," said Lucrezia. "I think you over-rate it. A good understanding is much rarer and more important." (p. 262)

Notes
1 Inaugural Linklater lecture, Aberdeen University, 1999

PRIVATE ANGELO: CHARACTERS

THE MEN

Angelo
Angelo is the prism through which we, the readers, are invited to view the war. With his immensely generous and kindly personality, the name seems well-chosen, his 'angelic' nature helping us in part accept the validity of his various comments. But it is above all his disarming honesty about his own lack of courage faced with the violence of the war machine that really helps persuade us that this honesty of vision might apply to his other perceptions.

Linklater uses Angelo to distil his own experiences of two wars into a clear-sighted view of how a country suffers not only from its occupiers but also through the actions of its liberators. Seeing the world from the viewpoint of an honest innocent has quite a tradition in literature. Most famous of all is the young man Candide in Voltaire's novella of the same name. Candide is someone whose clearness of vision punctures some of the accepted views of the world around him, just as Angelo's various verdicts on 'liberation' deflate any too uncritical a view of it. In an article he had written for Time and Tide in 1940 Linklater had shown his admiration for Jaroslav's Hasek's *The Good Soldier Schweik* which is a novel in which an innocent young soldier in the Austrian army of the First World War shows up the violent madness of war, much in the same way that Angelo does in the Second World War.

Linklater makes Angelo's condemnation of war all the more powerful by having him avoid for the most part violent outbursts of anger, preferring rather to have him underline war's idiocy by incisive wit.

Speaking of the forthcoming liberation of Pontefiore, Lucia, Lucrezia's sister, demands of Angelo:

"Are you not eager for it to be liberated?" asked Lucia.
"It is sometimes necessary to go to the dentist," said

Angelo, "but I have never seen anyone eager to go; and this is a more serious operation than the pulling of a tooth." (p. 173)

In the paragraphs that follow, Angelo gives a witty and ironic account of how occupier and liberator alike can destroy totally a village, the full accuracy of which is demonstrated only a few pages later when Pontefiore is razed to the ground. Linklater saves many of the novel's ironic criticisms of war for Angelo, but, ever the Scotsman, Linklater also uses him for sly observations on the English. The Count, puzzled by what he thinks might be English gunfire after the signing of the Armstice, consults Angelo who replies:

"They may not have heard about it," said Angelo. "The English are frequently unaware of what goes on in Europe." (p. 8)

This and Angelo's other enquiries and comments about aspects of English life, women and politics (pp. 85–86) provide Linklater with opportunities to satirise gently the Scots' southern neighbours. (Although these comments from the 'innocent' Angelo are always amusing, Linklater occasionally risks undermining the credibility of his character by placing in the mouth of an untravelled young Italian peasant remarks which, at times, may sound almost just too knowing.)

But as well as being the focus of much of the novel's humour, Angelo, in his enthusiastic embracing of all branches of creativity, stands as the antithesis of the destructive havoc that war represents. The sheer joy he finds in Piero della Francesca's *The Adoration of the Shepherds* highlights his belief in the nurturing power of art:

"There is more life and truth and beauty in this picture than you will find in forty living villages [...] We have a lot of bad company now in Italy, and therefore the greater need to associate with what is good." (p. 26)

This joy in art merges into a similar joy in the fertility and civilising beauty of the Tuscan landscape:

> As the little grapes in the valley are sweet already and coloured with their ripeness, so Tuscany wears its bloom and is plump as a young grape with sweetness [...] "The land is very ancient, yet summer comes to it with the colour of a new invention. When Rome was but an angry thought, we were civilised and had our arts, and when the world was in its dark despair we woke it with our painting and our poetry [...]" (p. 241)

Angelo's own 'dark despair' in time of war is lightened, above all, by his love of women in general and Lucrezia in particular. It is perhaps no surprise that at the novel's end Angelo's household contains not only his wife Lucrezia but the rescued Annunziata, both once victims of the destructive violence of war, but now living proof of his wholehearted dedication to creativity, for both are now pregnant ...

Reunited with his beloved Madonna from the *Adoration*, comforted in his prospering Tuscan farm by the love of Lucrezia and Annunziata, Angelo, in the novel's final pages, celebrates in full all the joy in life and beauty that drew Linklater himself to the irrepressible vitality and life-affirming forces of Italy.

Count Agesilas Piccologrando di Pontefiore

The Count, as well as being Angelo's patron and commanding officer as Colonel of the 914th Regiment of Tuscan Infantry (the Sucklings of the Wolf), is also, in all probability, his father. Although this is never explicitly stated, both the Count's devotion to the memory of Angelo's dead mother and certain personality traits which he shares with Angelo suggest a closer relationship than the novel openly admits.

In creating two key characters who represent opposites in several ways – youth and age, country and town, peasant and aristocrat, private and officer, innocence and experience – Linklater usefully employs the pairing to broaden the novel's canvas of wartime Italy. The name itself,

Piccologrando, – literally 'little/big' – captures the man's essence: he makes grand-sounding statements which are usually smaller in substance than their pompous words might suggest. His 'philosophising' is frequently merely self-justification of his actions or inactions. An instance of this is his hypocritical chastisement of Angelo for his lack of courage (p. 3) but, as it turns out, he, as the regiment's commanding officer, has never even seen the front line.

Like Angelo, he values art, but it is his appreciation of the monetary worth of his pictures which drives him to send them from Rome to Pontefiore where he is quite happy to conceal them from sight in a hiding place in the castle; Angelo cannot bear the idea that Piero della Francesca's *The Adoration of the Shepherds* should be 'imprisoned in darkness'. For the Count, art is of financial value, for Angelo it gives 'happiness and consolation'. (p. 26)

Like Angelo, he has an eye for the ladies. While Angelo ends up with two women in his life, the Count for some time, it seems, has split his life between his glamorous mistress, the Marchesa Dolce, who favours Rome, and his wife, the Yorkshire-born Countess who runs the estate at Pontefiore in the Count's absence. Given as he is more to philosophising than action, it is fortunate that both these very different women have strong practical streaks to look after both him and his interests.

Like Angelo, he faces problems in the matter of courage. Although he admonishes Angelo for his lack of courage, he has, hypocritically, led his regiment throughout the war from Rome. The announcement of the armistice gives him a certain rash confidence to confront (p. 10) a German commander but this is more an act of foolhardiness than one of courage since it leads to imprisonment, crippling financial blackmail and the impounding of his property.

Unlike Angelo, however, he is devious and corrupt, defrauding the Italian army by diverting their supplies to sell for his own profit (p. 15) and, after liberation, defrauding the American army with the aid of the black marketeer Sergeant Vespucci and indulging in doubtful art 'exchanges' with a corrupt American colonel. (p. 218)

Only when facing possible death at the hands of a German firing squad does he confront his own shortcomings, revealing an awareness of his past errors and, despite his own cosseted war, an awareness, too, of the real horrors of war and a certain shame at his failure to acknowledge them earlier. (p. 100) This moment of self-awareness sees the Count at his best but it is short-lived, and, as the liberation of Italy wreaks its heavy toll of casualties and destruction all around him, this likeable rogue resumes his old ways, thriving and prospering unscrupulously, brushing aside any setback along the way (p. 217) as merely an opportunity to 'philosophise'. Whatever he may lack in morality, he makes up for in resilience.

At the novel's conclusion, the appearance of this old-world aristocrat as the happy representative of an American sewing machine company usefully symbolises not simply the social upheaval delivered by war to society's old order but also the adaptability of Italians to confront the new one. Like Angelo, Don Agesilas has learnt 'the most useful of all accomplishments, which is to survive'. (p. 262)

THE WOMEN
Just as Angelo and the Count represent the people and the ruling class of Italy struggling to emerge from war, so, too, do we have a similar representative picture from the novel's women. Each exemplifies a different facet of the problems facing women when their men folk engage in warfare. From the elegant, worldly Marchesa Dolce to the homely but equally practical Emilia Bigi, all find their own ways to survive the brutality of warfare and to accommodate its privations. In his Introduction to the Canongate edition of the novel, Magnus Linklater, the author's son, comments that the novel's women seem:

> [...] undoubtedly the stronger, and certainly the more sensible sex. (p.viii)

This is a view fully endorsed by Lucrezia in dismissing Angelo's obsessive preoccupation with courage – or its absence – as thoroughly wrong-headed:

"Courage is a common quality in men of little sense," said Lucrezia. "I think you over-rate it. A good understanding is much rarer and more important." (p. 262)

Each of the novel's women has to learn to understand how to survive the man-made perils of warfare in her own context and in her own way, often at great cost and distress.

The Marchesa Dolce
Comfort-loving and dedicated to her own appearance though she may be (p. 90), the Marchesa is loyally devoted to the Count. She shows wily cunning in understanding the greed of the occupying Germans when she sets out to rescue him from imprisonment. Her sharp assessment of the situation (p. 33) shows a pragmatic mind at work behind 'the voluptuous quality of her admirable figure' (p. 32). We admire, too, her cool courage in concealing the Count under the cushions of her sofa when her home is raided by the Germans seeking the Count to appropriate yet more of his fortune. Ever the practical woman, she reprimands the Count for his indulgence in 'philosophising' on his release (p. 57, p. 91) and is more clear-sightedly critical than the Count when he attempts to praise Fascism. (p. 57) Like the Count, however, she clearly moves easily amongst the occupying and liberating powers (p. 33, p. 218) without suffering any of the personal vicissitudes of Lucrezia or Annunziata. Her loyalty is to the survival of herself and those close to her rather than to any cause as she socialises elegantly amongst the changing power bases in occupied and liberated Rome.

The Countess Piccologrando
Born a Miss Goodge in Bradford, the Count's wife is as different from the Marchesa as any two women could be, although both share a shrewd practicality in defending his interests. Lacking the glamour of his mistress as 'the prettiness of her girlhood had long since gone' (p. 21) she is driven by a sense of duty to protect, not only the Count's estate, but also the inhabitants of Pontefiore, prioritising their welfare even over her own feelings when news of the Count's 'death'

is announced. (p. 144) To this end, she had sent away all the young men of the village into the hills to avoid conscription by the Germans. (p. 150) Good-hearted as she may be, she clearly comes across to the villagers (p.144) and to her nephew Tom Trivet as somewhat severe and judgemental. (p. 147) Like the Marchesa, she shows the same cool courage under pressure, notably when the castle is taken over by boorish retreating German troops. Her composure is only shaken when the Germans destroy her cherished leather-bound copies of the novels of Ouida. The loss of these volumes reveal an emotional chink in the armour of a seemingly unemotional woman; she is devastated by what is a kind of violation of her inner life:

> The Countess whimpered like a child, and tears ran down her cheeks to her quivering mouth. (p. 161)

But like Lucrezia, following violation of the physical kind, she demonstrates resilience in adapting to this assault in her own fashion: the Countess takes to drink. The resulting mellowness sees her becoming a more tolerant figure who gains greatly in popularity amongst the villagers and who is viewed with increasing admiration by her husband. (p. 220)

Annunziata
While the other women are rooted in their various communities, Annunziata is different in that she represents the women displaced and set adrift by the hazards of war. Originally a married woman from Pesaro where she meets Angelo, she is widowed by the time they meet again eighteen months later, this time near Ravenna, where she is begging in the streets for food for herself and her baby. Her husband has been shot by the Germans and her subsequent Polish protector – and father of her baby – has disappeared in the chaos of war. For her liaison with a foreigner, Annunziata suffers the public humiliation of having her head shaved by Fascists-turned-Communists who 'wanted to do something to show they were now Patriots, and prove their enthusiasm.' (p. 235) In this darkest chapter of the novel (in which Angelo loses

his left hand) Linklater reminds us in the understated words of Annunziata that 'we are not all so good-humoured, we Italians, as we pretend to be'. (p. 235) Nevertheless, the goodheartedness of Angelo sees her installed comfortably, after a long series of sufferings, in his unconventional but loving household. Her fate personalises and parallels the buffeting of the nation as a whole as it struggles to survive the reversals of war and to re-shape its identity in the post-war world.

Lucrezia
Lucrezia embodies the age-old dilemma of women whose loved ones go off to war. Although not married to Angelo as the novel opens, she is his 'boyhood's sweetheart'. (p.16) Angelo, however, has been absent for three years and she has no way of knowing whether he is alive or dead. When the handsome and lonely Englishman, Tom Trivet, arrives, she becomes involved with him and has his child, Tommaso, although the relationship does not appear to be deep or long-lasting. On the return of Angelo, we see the internal division in her response:

> [...] joy had flushed Lucrezia's cheeks and lighted her eyes when she first saw Angelo, and she had made a swift movement as though she meant to run straight into his arms. But then she halted [...] and her eyes grew round with fear, and she lifted a hand to her mouth like a child restraining a cry of pain. (p. 25)

There is genuine joy at his return and real fear that her secret will emerge. When Angelo is anxious for them to marry, she rationalises away marriage in time of war for she has no desire to 'be a wife for two or three weeks [...] and then be left alone'. (p. 30) Of course, marriage would also oblige her to explain the existence of Tommaso as part of her close family circle. When there is an eventual exposition of her secret, Lucrezia is unapologetic, making a feisty defence of her behaviour, pointing out that she had felt 'sorry for Trivet in his loneliness' (p. 187), although also admitting under cross-examination by Angelo to finding him attractive:

"Do you think I would have misbehaved with anyone whose appearance was repulsive? I am not so wicked as that, I hope. Trivet has good features, white teeth, and truly handsome eyes." (p. 187)

While there is a claim to moral justification in her answers there is also an admission of human weakness, too. She attempts to rationalise her personal desires as coinciding with decent behaviour, in a way that is not unreminiscent of the Count when obliged to explain his own equivocal behaviour. The problem for Angelo is similar to the problem of the reader: how are we to judge such behaviour? There is no final answer; Lucrezia's plea is that the charitable aspect of her behaviour should be favoured over more ungenerous interpretations:

"If a woman pleads that charity was the motive," said Lucrezia, "it shows that she is aware of the high place that charity should have in life [...] She has the seeds of virtue in her, if not virtue itself, because she knows the poor world's need of charity." (p. 188)

Given what we have seen in this novel of the destructive violation of a country and the humiliating rape of the individual, the 'poor world' does desperately need charity and Lucrezia's claim has to be given considerable weight in arriving at any verdict. For Lucrezia's fate parallels the fate of Italy: both have been viciously violated and both respond with generosity of spirit to the outcome of the rape: Lucrezia cherishing little Othello as much as any of his half-siblings; the residents of Pontefiore setting about the rebuilding of their lives with resilience, optimism and an absence of bitterness. Outspoken and spirited, she has none of the self-doubts of her husband and, in her – finally – warm acceptance of Annunziata and the other women in their household, she represents the spirit of tolerance and reconciliation in the new Italy.

THE DARK OF SUMMER: INTRODUCTION

Published in 1956, *The Dark of Summer* is a complex novel whose experimental structure gave Linklater considerable trouble in writing. While selling well, it received little serious attention from the heavyweight literary critics of the time at the time or, indeed, since. Allan Massie, however, in his introduction to the Canongate edition describes it as Linklater's 'masterpiece'.

Within the novel's own ambitious structure there is a further complication: a convoluted family history, *The Wishart Inheritance*, which Linklater skilfully uses to underpin several of the novel's major themes. Adding still more to the novel's narrative ambition is its sweep in time and place which carries the reader from the Shetlands of the Jacobite Rebellion of 1745 to the Supreme Headquarters of the Allied Powers in Europe (SHAPE), part of NATO in post-World War II Europe. The novel follows a cyclical progress, beginning where it ends in Shetland, but in the interval takes us to the Faeroes, North Africa, Italy, Korea, Japan, Singapore and Paris.

Guiding us through these complexities of time and place is the hero, Tony Chisholm, whom Linklater's biographer, Michael Parnell describes as a 'rather humourless, pedestrian narrator'.[1] This is a charge which perhaps requires further examination since Linklater's approach to character revelation here is – intriguingly – rather similar to that of Chisholm's novelist mother who is described as treating

> "[...] people, and situations, too, as if they were onions. She peels them. Peel after peel comes away – you had no idea there were so many [...] And at last, when you think there's nothing left, she exposes the heart of the situation."
> (**C** p. 179, **B** p. 189)

This is a comment which illuminates both Linklater's presentation of Chisholm's character and the novel's narrative progress through personal, family and national history. Chisholm may never develop a sense of humour, but seeing him work stoically through his various tribulations humanises him in a way that invites our involvement. As the novel advances we are intrigued to learn more and more of Chisholm, whose self-doubts, personal and family secrets emerge only gradually, as does our final understanding of certain of the novel's narrative strands. For here, too, the immediate surface appearance does not always reflect underlying reality. It is a novel which makes us wait for 'the heart of the situation'.

The danger of jumping to judgments which are too clear-cut and apparent is something which Linklater warns us against in the very opening paragraphs of the novel. Speaking of the Shetland landscape on mid-summer evenings, he comments:

> The landscape becomes an image of the world in which we live. It is not dark, but nothing can be seen as plainly and decisively as the light of noon pretends – noon flatters and deludes us – yet all that can be seen is solid, solid enough for faith, and if one's heart is whole one can enjoy the beauty inherent in our mystery – a beauty that is, paradoxically, more visible in half-light. (**C** p. 1, **B** p. 1)

Here he is warning us that a rush to seek overly straightforward answers to moral questions may provide answers which are as harsh and unrefined as the light at noon. He uses this 'half-light' (the 'dark' of the novel's title) as a metaphor for a more reliable interpretation. Just as it is only in the subtlety of the half-light during the summer twilight that we can fully appreciate the full beauty of the contours of the landscape, so too do we need a more nuanced perspective on human behaviour and motivation to respond to its twists and turns with full understanding. Provided, of course, he adds, that our heart is 'whole' as we observe it. What Linklater means by 'whole' and how his hero arrives at this wholeness furnishes the novel with its philosophical and narrative thrust.

It is no coincidence that in the opening paragraphs Linklater seeks to link geographical landscape with the human condition, for throughout the novel we note that scenic descriptions find parallels in the hero's psychological landscapes. As we have seen, the opening paragraphs find Chisholm 'skin tight with love' and 'whole', a condition which is mirrored in the radiantly beautiful twilight of summer nights in Shetland. Similarly, the novel's great descriptive set-piece – the storm at sea in Chapter Six – foreshadows the cataclysmic mental torment Chisholm undergoes when he feels he has been responsible for the death of Wishart and the orphaning of his children in the following scenes. His resulting guilt is a crippling force on his personality. It literally destroys his will to live, pitching him into a mental state which finds a geographic resonance only when his war career takes him to the barren landscape of the North African desert. Here his depressed state of mind is further intensified by news of the suicide of his wife. The sterility of the landscape here matches the sterility of his present inner life. Although physically wounded in Italy, Chisholm's spiritual state improves gradually amidst scenery which he describes as 'magnificent'. Later in the novel, the bleakness of Korea matches the grimness of his mood where he has to face the death of Olaf Wishart in that 'stricken land' where 'the lethal malignity of the Siberian wind' debilitated both body and spirit. It is only in Paris in the spring that we see Chisholm restored to full spiritual health when nature's rebirth seems to promote his own spiritual renaissance:

> This was the renewal of life: the bright air proclaimed it, green leaves announced it, and every crowded pavement acknowledged it. (C p. 234, B p. 247)

Only now does Chisholm feel himself 'whole', ready for marital happiness with Gudrun. The novel's narrative takes the reader on a lengthy global journey, mirroring the long spiritual journey that Chisholm has to undertake to reach 'wholeness'. It is testimony to Linklater's artistry that these parallels are never thrust at the reader, but their presence enriches enormously the reading experience by discreetly situating Chisholm's changing psychological states through various geographical positionings.

A chapter in Chisholm's wartime wanderings takes him to the Faeroes, where Linklater's talents as landscape painter are seen at their most vivid in depicting this virtually unknown theatre of war:

> The smoke above Tórshaven, when we sailed in the ebbing of the dark, was like incense rising from a vulgar but faithful altar – an altar in a wilderness of ocean – and among the northern fjords the blowing peat-reek of a solitary chimney seemed to be the assertion of human hope against geology's excommunication. (C p. 57, B p. 58–59)

Equally peripheral to many readers' knowledge is the shadowy figure Vidkun Quisling who, while he never appears, is clearly a close associate of the novel's anti-hero, Mungo Wishart. But he is much more than a plot device to implicate Wishart in treason, for he underpins one of the novel's main themes – that of betrayal.

Vidkun Quisling (the exact nature of whose treachery would have been more familiar to Linklater's generation than ours) was the puppet ruler of Norway for Hitler for most of the war period. The name 'quisling' has become a synonym for a traitor, but Vidkun Quisling (1887–1945) was not always seen in this light. Working as a diplomat in Russia during the twenties with the distinguished Norwegian explorer, humanitarian and Nobel peace prize laureate Fridtjof Nansen (1861–1930), Quisling looked after British interests in Moscow at a time when Britain had no diplomatic relations with the Soviet Union. For this he was awarded the CBE (Commander of the British Empire), an honour which was hastily rescinded once his Nazi leanings became fully apparent. Before his conversion to Nazisim, however, he had been a distinguished mathematician and had worked with Nansen to aid the plight of people displaced by the First World War. Piecing this information together with his admittedly vague aspirations in this novel, we can deduce that he is used by Linklater as a symbol of multiple betrayals: that of his own one-time principles, that of his former British colleagues, that of his own nation and eventually even of Hitler himself, for history does seem to confirm that he foresaw early on the collapse of the Third Reich and entertained ideas, like Mungo Wishart, that the Norse races could become progenitors of a new, revitalised Northern Europe. Like Wishart, too, he is seen to epitomise the dangers of certainties and extreme convictions. Quisling and Wishart stand as the novel's polar opposites of Chisholm. As Silver exclaims on hearing of the fate of Olaf Wishart who died in battle attempting to expiate his father's guilt:

> "Oh, God damn Mungo Wishart and all those bloody egotists who take up causes!" (**C** p. 207, **B** p. 219)

Tony Chisholm is a far cry from being a man of convictions, certainties or causes, groping as he does towards a vision of living that resolves the questionings and self-doubts that existence poses in an imperfect world. Like *Private Angelo*, this is a novel about the individual trying to make sense of himself and his situation in war and its aftermath. Major world events sweep the heroes of both novels along, causing them mental turmoil and physical distress (albeit with important differences in tone and authorial voice). Finally, they both arrive at their own salvation, freed from the destructive forces – external and internal – which threatened to destroy them. Far from the theatres of action, they find a private peace, physically maimed but spiritually intact.

Notes
1 Parnell 1984:301

THE DARK OF SUMMER: SYNOPSIS

Chapter One
Tony Chisholm, the novel's one-armed hero, is out walking with his wife of twelve months one summer evening when they discover the remains of a body in construction works on land near their Shetland home. They both suspect it is the body of Old Dandy, a distant relative of Tony's wife, Gudrun. Old Dandy had disappeared over two hundred years previously, leaving behind a troubled family history which had embittered ever since the Wishart family in general and Gudrun's father in particular. In looking for proof of the corpse's identity, Tony cuts his hand on a dagger embedded in the body and, highly sensitive to any damage to his remaining hand, is driven to Lerwick by his wife to have the wound seen to by a doctor friend at a local hospital. The dazzling hospital lights remind Tony of similar lights which he had encountered during his war-time army career where the next chapter opens.

Chapter Two
It is a late winter's afternoon in the wartime London of 1941, twelve years previously. Chisholm has been summoned for a briefing on a mission to the War Office in Whitehall where, under the harsh lights of an underground office, he meets Pelly, an acquaintance from school, towards whom Chisholm feels a certain antipathy, fuelled by Pelly's reference to the death of Chisholm's younger brother, Peter. Chisholm is resentful of what he feels is Pelly's false sympathy. Chisholm's pain is such that the full story of Peter's death is not made entirely clear but it appears that he had been shot by a senior officer to halt panic spreading amongst other soldiers, hinting that Peter had behaved inappropriately in the face of the enemy, a fact that Chisholm does not like to admit to himself. Outside, in the winter's dusk, he covers his own pain by taking pity on two old women, one of whom had just lost her third son to the war effort. Later, in his club, he dines with a fellow club-member who cannot get over the memory of how his wife had been betrayed and lampooned

by young writers whom she had befriended. Pain of several kinds unites the chapter's three incidents.

Chapter Three
Subsequent to his Whitehall briefing, Tony sets off on the first of the novel's many journeys, initially to Edinburgh on a night train. During the night he reflects on his family: his VC-decorated father, killed in a glider accident, his flamboyant mother and his brother, Peter, for whom he feels such mixed emotions. Peter, handsome and intelligent, seems, however, in Tony's eyes to have lacked the necessary qualities for a military career but pushed himself to join the Territorial Army before being shot by his company commander, Cromar, for what appears to be cowardice in the face of the enemy. Admitting the memory of this brings terrible pain to Tony who is physically sick in contemplating it. Arriving in Edinburgh, he makes his way to Donisbristle where he boards a small plane for Kirkwall before boarding a drifter for the voyage to the northern town of Lyness. There he meets with an Intelligence Officer who briefs him on his mission to the Faeroes where he is to meet with two acquaintances who have a strange tale to tell the British authorities.

Chapter Four
Journeying to the Faeroes, Chisholm reflects on the ties of friendship and those of country and he is clear in his mind that should these acquaintances (met during an earlier visit to the islands in the spring of that same year) prove enemies to Britain, he would have no compunction in handing them over to the authorities. At the time of his first visit, Military Intelligence had invited him to make the acquaintances of these men and give his opinion of them. He had enjoyed the company of Bomlo and Torur and found them guilty of nothing worse than outspoken Faroese nationalism. The captain on this voyage is a Lieutenant Silver, a man of taste, lively mind and decisive opinions, whose strength of character Chisholm admires and to whom he is tempted to unburden himself over the matter of his brother but resists. Chisholm's tendency to

guard the privacy of his interior life is further underlined when he mentions another topic he would like to broach with the clear-thinking Silver: the matter of his adulterous wife – but he again resists the temptation.

Chapter Five
The Intelligence Officer he meets in Torshavn outlines the story of Bomlo and Torur: a boat had beached near Torur's home with two dead and three dying men aboard, apparently political refugees from Nazi-dominated Norway and victims of the cruel weather conditions. Given Bomlo's knowledge of Norwegian and the fact he had previously interrogated other refugees to ensure none were Nazi agents, Torur had informed Bomlo of this event, but not the authorities themselves. A hostile neighbour of Torur's, claimed after the death of all five that there had been a sixth man who had come ashore, a fact which Torur had not reported. Shortly afterwards, Bomlo and Torur were thought to be in possession of strictly rationed alcohol: could there be a connection? Chisholm is there to investigate. Knowing the two men socially, he feels somewhat embarrassed at his mission and is grateful for the company of the sharp-witted Silver on the voyage to his semi-official meeting with them. Hoping to keep his investigation low-keyed, Chisholm goes ashore, accompanied only by a shrewd Sergeant Fergusson. Armed with whisky, he is warmly welcomed by the two men, already slightly the worse of alcohol. They ramble on about a great re-birth of the northern nations after the war. Cleverly, Chisholm asks them if the men who came ashore gave them that idea. The mood changes and the men appear defensive. Changing the subject, they enquire how Tony acquired his Military Cross (yet another fact about Chisholm the reader is surprised to learn), offering their tale in return for his. Chisholm, terrified by approaching tanks at Dunkirk, had been frozen to the spot and had not retired with the rest of his men and had fought on, giving his company valuable time to retreat. Chisholm, however, views his actions as cowardice, seeing parallels with the story of his brother but with a much different outcome. Torur and Bomlo honour their promise and

take Chisholm to an outhouse where he finds a dead man is tied to a chair, the sixth man from the boat.

A confused tale now emerges. This man, Jon Jonsson, had persuaded Torur to hide him, saying he had come as a peace emissary from Vidkun Quisling, the Nazi puppet ruler of Norway, who now foresaw German defeat and was keen to talk to the British authorities. Initially impressed by Jonsson, Torur and Bomlo lose their respect when he attempts to bribe them to take him to Shetland to meet a good friend of Quisling's, seeing themselves being treated as accessories to spying rather than being respected as Faroese nationalists. Tying him up seated in a chair, they leave him in an outhouse where he dies in the night from the cold. It is the pragmatic Silver who later suggests the body should be shipped to Lyness with all its possessions and the matter left to the Intelligence Officer.

Chapter Six
Feeling out of his depth, Chisholm is only too happy to let Silver take charge of the move of the body to the ship. On board, Silver, musing over the unusual name Vidkun, remembers when in Norway in grand company he had heard someone remark on the presence of Vidkun 'with his English friend', someone of distinctive appearance according to Silver. He recounts that on a recent visit to Shetland he had seen that friend of Vidkun's again, identified now as a Mr Wishart. He presumes that this is the man that Jonsson was attempting to contact. Silver proposes that they invent an engine problem and go ashore near Wishart's house, Weddergarth, to investigate this possible link between a British subject and the Nazi puppet ruler of Norway. Sailing to Shetland they encounter a fierce storm at sea (one of the novel's set-pieces of description) which produces a real steering problem requiring attention and it is with some difficulty that they even make it to Weddergarth where Chisholm proposes to go ashore and invite Wishart aboard. On his walk there, still feeling ill after the effects of the storm, he encounters two children, a boy of around nine, Olaf, and a girl of about eleven, Gudrun, in front of whom Chisholm is violently sick.

They take pity on him and offer to take him to their father, Mungo Wishart. Weakened and ill, he is persuaded to stay the night.

Chapter Seven
As reading matter for the night, Gudrun gives Chisholm a privately published family history written by Mungo. In it we learn not only of the embittered family history (going back to the days of Old Dandy whose body was found at the novel's start) but also of the similarly embittered state of mind of Mungo Wishart whose hates encompass past members of his own family, his fellow Shetlanders and British governments whom he feels have betrayed nations around the world. These are all memories of betrayal of which Wishart cannot let go and has had them formalised in this publication. Chisholm, however, is convinced he is no German spy but rather a deeply unhappy and slightly unbalanced believer in the same somewhat far-fetched idea he had heard from Bomlo and Torur: that the world's morally bankrupt state would never improve until some form of Norse renaissance regenerated global morality.

Chapter Eight
After breakfast with Mrs Wishart and the two children to whom Chisholm warms greatly, he departs for the ship and there tells Silver of his belief that Wishart is no spy. Silver is unconvinced and suggests they invite Wishart to the ship for some discreet interrogation. Things go well until Silver invites Wishart to view their 'prisoner' in the hope that with his Norwegian connections Wishart might recognise him. Wishart downplays his Norwegian connections but agrees. Seeing the 'prisoner' is a corpse, he manifests outrage and storms off.

Silver is somewhat shamefaced and both men prepare for their interview with the Intelligence Officer and his commanding officer on Orkney. On the voyage Chisholm continues his reading of the tortured Wishart family history which records how the family was much impoverished by generations of lawyers attempting to establish the rival claims of Wishart and Pitcairn heirs to Old Dandy's estate. Once arrived, Chisholm and Silver report their findings, acknowledging some embarrassment in returning a corpse to Orkney as 'evidence'. Their excuse was that Silver was acting out a hunch that might elicit some evidence of guilt from Wishart, but clearly, they now feel, a mistake in judgment may have been made. The Commander reveals, however, that he, too, had been taking an interest in Wishart and that the latter had committed suicide the night of their interview. In his possession were poison capsules from German chemists and, in his grate, a pile of ashes of correspondence ...

Chapter Nine
While acknowledging Wishart's probable treason, Chisholm is burdened by his guilt at his part in his death and applies for a posting in North Africa, hoping to get himself killed. Arriving in Cairo he meets up again with Pelly who is kind to him, appearing to regret having told Tony the truth concerning his brother Peter's death. Impatient to join his division in the desert, he takes off and is quickly caught up in action leading to the battle of El Alamein. Coming under fire from German tanks, he is astonished at the bravery of a nameless soldier who loses his life in attempting to rescue Chisholm. Chisholm is lightly wounded. In the succeeding five months, however, this event and the comradeship of his fellow-soldiers brings around changes in his outlook and his death-wish is finally banished when he comes close to death itself at Wadi Akarit. This is quickly followed by being drafted by Pelly into planning the Sardinian landings. He learns without any emotion other than that of relief of the suicide of his unfaithful wife who we discover had had an affair with his brother Peter.

Chapter Ten
This chapter finds Chisholm as part of the war campaign in Italy where he spends the next year, arriving in September 1943 (the date of the opening of *Private Angelo*). By his own confession, he seems in a much more stable frame of mind after the traumas of Shetland and North Africa. While enjoying

his work as a quartermaster, he comes across a cousin of Silver's, Poynter, in whom he sees parallels with his dead brother and concerns for his welfare begin to trouble him as they had done for Peter. In seeking information on Poynter's welfare he comes across a wounded young officer who speaks of Poynter only with contempt yet hero-worships the behaviour of a colonel who turns out to be the same Cromar who had Tony's brother shot. Tony is disturbed by trying to reconcile this picture of Cromar (who gave his life for his men) with his own severe judgment of the man. Shortly afterwards, working with his men on a supply convoy, Tony casts caution to the winds and spontaneously races to help his wounded colleagues when they come under attack from German guns. He is wounded and hospitalised.

Chapter Eleven
During this hospitalisation with a broken leg, Chisholm reflects on the behaviour that had driven him to abandon what he calls his own coldness and caution of nature to help others in distress. Now he understands the compassion of the nameless soldier in Chapter 9 and of Cromar, who had both given their lives to help others and seems delighted that he, the most self-critical of men, can manifest some of the same compassion by reacting spontaneously to help others in distress. Although he confesses that no one had been saved by his action, the discovery of the existence of this heretofore unsuspected compassion in him boosts his morale immeasurably and he now feels 'whole' for the first time. Respecting himself just a little more now, he allows himself to fall mildly in love with the succession of nurses who seem to like him with his new 'openness to life'. Interrupting this period of new-found self-respect is the re-appearance of Silver as a fellow patient. He, too, has changed, but not for the better in Chisholm's eyes. He has a new cynicism, believing that Britain's war is driven only by the need for survival rather than any question of moral principle. Although decorated for courageous behaviour, he seems contemptuous both of his own war effort and that of his country, talking of starting afresh by going to work in the Far East. He returns

Tony's copy of Wishart's book which had been left aboard in Shetland. Tony discovers the passage where Wishart rails against 'the evil clouds of poisoned memory' which, in his opinion, blights hopelessly the life of men and nations. Chisholm delves back into his own 'poisoned memory' when he hears of the death of his mother whom, it now emerges, he had judged to be guilty of adultery, thus casting a shadow over his previously improving mental state. Talk of Wishart reveals that Chisholm has been corresponding with Gudrun Wishart.

Chapter Twelve
The end of the war finds Chisholm in London where, meeting Charles Aytoun, his mother's former lover, he reveals to Aytoun and the reader a little more of his philosophy of life. Although not at ease with the post-war socialist world, he is a little more at ease with himself, thanks, he confesses, to the more positive reflections on his personality that his second wound had engendered in him. It is now with more self-confidence that he takes up his position as a 29-year-old Lieutenant Colonel in Austria. Posted to the East on the outbreak of the Korean War, he runs into Olaf Wishart, now a volunteer Ulster Rifleman, for whom he feels protective through guilt at his role in the elder Wishart's death. Gudrun, he learns, is in her final year at university. Olaf and Tony are wounded on the battlefield, Olaf fatally, Tony losing his left arm. The dying Olaf asks if his death 'will make up for him'. It later becomes clear that his volunteering came about as a result of his shame at discovering that his father was seen as being a spy. Hospitalised in Singapore, Tony is visited by Silver who seeks to employ Tony in his successful Far Eastern business. Tony is tempted but his sense of obligation to his country (although he does not approve of much being carried out by the socialist government) finally triumphs. Informed of Olaf's motivation for volunteering, Silver also confesses to having had a certain feeling of guilt in Mungo Wishart's death but now having Wishart's betrayal of his country confirmed by Olaf's death, this guilt is commuted to pity for Olaf.

Chapter Thirteen

Much of the final chapter involves Tony's visit to Shetland to tell Mrs Wishart the circumstances of Olaf's death. He is met at the airport by a very grown-up, smart Gudrun. Arriving at Weddergarth, he is struck both by the appearance of Mrs Wishart, changed by the double tragedy of a lost husband and son, and the more prosperous appearance of the estate. Gudrun explains that the former dilapidated state of the place was due to her father's extravagance and that under the more sensible, practical management of her mother their finances had improved. Gudrun confirms that she and Olaf were both aware that their father had committed suicide, and had not died of heart failure as had been put about at the time. They were also made painfully aware at school that their father had been a spy, resulting in Olaf's tragic decision to volunteer to help expiate his father's guilt. Tony is embarrassed by the part played by him in her father's suicide but Gudrun assures him that they had never regarded the ill Tony in this light, blaming rather Silver. After his appointment to the Joint Services Staff College, Tony returns to Shetland and the Wisharts where he is made very welcome and an attraction grows up between him and Gudrun, blighted, however, by Chisholm's guilt by his part in her father's death. Around this time, influenced by a fisherman's remark on the drive of trout to swim upstream to breed, Tony has a dream in which it becomes clear to him that if we see ourselves like the fish swimming upstream, allowing the opposing current to carry away our troubling memories, we shall finally be free of the bitterness which these recurring thoughts engendered in Mungo Wishart. In this way, he sees his way clear to drawing closer to Gudrun with whom he resumes a warm correspondence. Posted to NATO headquarters, he visits Paris in the spring where the beauty of the city, the season and the general joy in life experienced by those around him confirm his exhilaration in the new possibilities in life. He returns to Shetland, proposes to Gudrun and is accepted. The novel, having performed a circle in time and place, returns to its point of departure.

THE DARK OF SUMMER: THEMES

The corrosive power of memory
The novel turns on its head the idea from Wordsworth's ode 'Intimations of Immortality' that our memory harbours traces of a happy pre-birth existence in heaven:

> Not in entire forgetfulness,
> And not in utter nakedness,
> But trailing clouds of glory do we come
> From God, who is our home. (ll. 63–66)

Events which befall Tony Chisholm, Mungo Wishart and Olaf Wishart in this novel suggest that memory, far from being a happy reminder of our divine origins, is a curse.

It is Mungo Wishart's inability to forget his own shameful family history of double-dealing and what he sees as Britain's unprincipled behaviour in its past dealings with Ireland and the nations of the Near East which embitter his mind to the point that he develops 'the madness of a fixed idea' (p.123), leading him to dabble in doubtful dealings with the Norwegian Nazi Vidkun Quisling. Suspecting his treachery has been discovered, he commits suicide. In his family memoir he refers to the Wordsworth quotation, adding

> "But they are no clouds of glory we drag behind us. They are the black and evil clouds of poisoned memory. Memory is the curse of man, the curse of nations. No man who remembers, no country that can never forget, has ever lived happily or ever will." (**C** pp. 175–76, **B** p. 186)

Ironically, he cannot apply this insight to his own miserable life, being a helpless prisoner and victim of 'poisoned memory'.

For much of the novel, Tony Chisholm, too, is someone who is plagued by the unhappiness of memory. Initially we hear how the memory of his VC father's success is a constant reminder of his own inadequacies, undermining an already poor self-image. As the novel advances we hear gradually of more memories which fill him with shame and despair: his brother Peter has been shot for cowardice in the face of the enemy; Chisholm's wife has been unfaithful with many men (including Peter); he harbours memories of his own mother's unfaithfulness. More importantly for his own lasting happiness, his guilt at the memory of the part he played in Mungo Wishart's death prevents him for a time sealing his relationship with Gudrun.

It is only late in the novel that a dream after a day's fishing allows him to see that 'memory is not inseparable' (p231) from the human mind if we, like breeding trout, go against the river of time's flow. Memory, if allowed to do so, will accompany us downstream, bearing all our unhappy memories with us through life; but, when we do not allow ourselves to be swept along with them but strive against the flow, we can detach from ourselves the bitterness of memory.

> [...] the up-stream swimmer and the spawning fish can shed their yesterdays. (**C** p. 231, **B** p. 245)

It is only when he makes this discovery that Tony eventually frees himself from the debilitating miseries of memory that have plagued his life.

Memory has much more tragic implications for young Olaf Wishart, who, deeply conscious of the shameful memory of his father's actions, seeks to expiate that memory by volunteering for the Korean war, and thus is killed.

Minor characters, too, like the old Liberal MP at Button's club where Chisholm dines also suffer from the demons of memory, this latter unable to forget the public lampooning of his wife by writers to whom she had been kind:

> His wife had been dead for several years, and the injury done to her had become, in him, a deepening wound. It had become incurable, because he could not forget it ...
> (**C** p. 23, **B** p. 23)

This 'deepening wound' of memory is finally cured in Chisholm, not simply by the vision in his dream but also by the pragmatism of his wife Gudrun who, although Mungo Wishart's daughter has inherited much of the common sense of her mother and can put her past hatred of her father's actions behind her:

"I shan't make the mistake he did, and let hate poison me. He was a miserable man; poor father, and I'm never going to think of him again, if I can help it." (**C** p. 221, **B** p. 234)

It is only when freed from the burden of memory that Linklater's characters have here any hope of peace or happiness. In the world of Chisholm and his associates, memory is a destructive malignity.

Betrayal
Closely linked to the idea of the misery-inducing powers of memory is the theme of betrayal, for many of the destructive memories derive from what is felt to be betrayal at familial or national level.

Mungo Wishart considers his betrayal of his country as justified as a result of what he sees as Lloyd George's betrayal of Armenia, Azerbaijan, Georgia and various other nations of the Caucasus, to say nothing of what he felt was British perfidy in dealing with Ireland. (Adding to this political dimension are the much less equivocal betrayals of Vidkun Quisling: of his nation and even, here, the mooted betrayal of his one-time ally, Hitler.)

At a historical level, we have the betrayal of the Jacobite Old Dandy by Wishart's 18th-century ancestors, on the pretext of what they in turn call Dandy's 'betrayal' of the Hanoverian king in the '45 rebellion.

Also to be considered are the multiple betrayals in Chisholm's life we have already noted: that by his brother with Tony's wife, the many betrayals by the same woman with other lovers and, in addition, there is the betrayal of his father by his mother with her lover, Charles Aytoun.

What is interesting in the novel, however, is the response of the injured party in each case. Wishart and Chisholm diverge dramatically in the ways they confront betrayal. Mungo

Wishart, enraged, resorts to treachery as a result of what he sees as betrayal by Britain, thus poisoning not only his entire existence but leading directly to his death and, indirectly, to the death of his son Olaf (Old Dandy, too, rails loudly against his betrayal by the Wisharts and ends up with a dagger in his ribs, and is thrown into a peat-bog and forgotten about for two hundred years ...).

Chisholm, for his part, stoically works his way through the weight of victimhood as he defends his country in war, until a realisation towards the novel's close allows him to shuffle off the burden of the betrayals which have beset him. Tony's ability to dedicate his social action to a cause greater than himself (however great his sense of personal betrayal) sees him finally rewarded with a satisfying sense of worth in the new, post-war Europe of the North Atlantic Treaty:

> I was now a servant, not only of the Queen, but of the United States and Luxembourg, of Greece and Turkey, of France and Iceland and all the other signatories of the Treaty. It was, from the beginning, an exhilarating feeling [...] I felt as never before the importance of being a soldier in this make-or-mar century. (C p. 232, B p. 245–46)

Tony's final happiness and sense of fulfilment derive from his refusal to become embittered or disaffected by betrayal, persevering in his own loyalties, however painful the process, to a cause greater than himself and thereby ultimately freeing himself from the weight of multiple betrayals.

The transforming power of war
Almost the entire novel takes place in a world at war. War is seen as a powerful transforming force on men's conduct, often ennobling previously unremarkable lives at moments of great danger but occasionally also exposing underlying weaknesses, hidden in peacetime.

Peter Chisholm, Tony's brother, well illustrates this latter point. In peace time, he had been an attractive if weak character, but placed under the pressure of war and army life, his fragile personality had collapsed totally and his cowardly behaviour under fire had led to his death at the hand of Cromar. We later learn that Tony himself, when placed in a similarly terrifying position had emerged with a Military Cross, despite being of the same fearful nature as his brother. This causes him to wonder how in the same heat of battle, men's behaviour can be so disparate:

> I was secretly pleased with myself – pleased, that is, with the discipline that had let me recover from a moment of panic which might have earned me, as it earned Peter, a bullet in the back – (C p. 65, B p. 67)

Tony witnesses a further example of the transfiguring power of war when he is rescued in North Africa by an unknown, foul-mouthed soldier who later dies in attempting to rescue another of Tony's companions. This selfless action by a very ordinary soldier to a complete stranger shakes him to the core:

> Why had he done it?
> Why, for the sake of two strangers, had he risked his life, and lost it? Pity, I suppose, but why should pity move a man so strongly? I heard, in memory, the coarseness of his anger when he felt in him the compulsion of pity: he had gone to his death – for a stranger – with the soldier's word on his lips. He was a man of slovenly appearance, and probably of slovenly habit. (C p. 153, B p. 164)

There is a second, even more powerful example of how war can, if not perhaps change a person, at least change how that person is viewed. This occurs later in Italy when Chisholm learns that Cromar, his brother's executioner, whom he judged 'a man of perverse stupidity' had given his life heroically to save the lives of an endangered battalion. For the moment he cannot reconcile his previous view of Cromar with

> [...] this self-sacrificing man who, in his final revelation, was moved by a compassion so extreme that sympathy grew

hot as wrath, and who died in a wrath of love? For surely this was the truth, the motive and cause of his behaviour ... (**C** p. 167, **B** p. 177)

(We here now have a better understanding of Chisholm's warning in the first paragraphs of the novel of the dangers of leaping to moral judgements too hastily 'in the light of noon' which in its harshness, he claims, 'deludes us'. Here, verdicts on character are seen to require the more nuanced light of lived experience – 'the dark of summer' of the novel's title.)

Shortly after this encounter with the unnamed soldier, Tony discovers part of the answer to some of the mystery of man's behaviour when, witnessing a German attack on an Allied convoy on an Italian bridge, he, without thinking, throws himself in front of the guns to rescue a screaming driver and

> with the vision in my mind – the intolerable vision – of men trapped and bleeding in the wreckage of their lorries, I ran towards the bridge. (**C** p. 169, **B** p. 179)

It is with some surprise that Chisholm discovers that he, too, like the unnamed soldier and Cromar, has depth of compassion in him which he had not realised:

> [...] I could not realize that compassion was their only motive, because I had not known the strength of compassion, and in the narrowness of my spirit I had been unwilling to admit the possibility of its strength. But now I knew.
> (**C** p. 170, **B** p. 180)

Chisholm is confronted with the paradox that the awfulness of war can, on occasions, transform behaviour and men in a way that underlines fundamental but unsuspected goodness.

Olaf Wishart is another character who sees war's power to transform. Unlike Tony, he has no fundamental weakness in his own character to overcome; his presence in Korea seems driven by a desire to exorcise the guilt he feels about his father. He appears to have volunteered for the Korean War to commute a family legacy of shame into one of which he might feel more proud. In so doing, however, he is fatally wounded. Dying, he whispers to Chisholm:

"Do you think – this – will make up – for him?"
(C p. 199, B p. 211)

War will allow Olaf, he hopes, the opportunity to offset his father's shame by fighting in the army of the country his father sought to betray. The fact that the once troubled Olaf now dies 'with a look of peace' on his face would appear to suggest that the expiation of his father's guilt is complete in his own mind, although the price of this transformation is his own life.

The transforming power of war is not restricted to the depiction of individual characters. While Linklater is far from glorifying war, he admits to its quietly edifying influence on the general population also. Embarking at King's Cross station for Edinburgh, Tony comments of his fellow war-time travellers, freely acknowledging their often rowdy drunken behaviour, yet adding:

We had a sense of purpose, a feeling of community, and what was patently unendurable we sustained by sympathy with, and pity for, the uncomplaining, shoulder-rubbing multitude [...] Patriotism was in ill repute – there were few, on the frontier of conscience, who would have declared patriotism in their baggage – but pity was evident on every platform. (C p. 24, B p. 26).

Bravery, fear, cowardice, compassion, expiation – all are present in Linklater's clear-eyed yet compassionate exploration of how war can touch otherwise ordinary lives, transforming them out of their unremarkable norms into greater or lesser versions of themselves.

THE DARK OF SUMMER: CHARACTERS

Tony Chisholm
The novel begins and ends with a narrator who, despite the loss of his arm, sees himself as being 'whole' and 'skin-tight with love' for his new wife, Gudrun. In between, however, we meet a Tony who is far from whole, one who has a strong sense of worthlessness and who is haunted by memories of various betrayals and family troubles. For a narrator, Chisholm is singularly reluctant to talk about himself and it is only gradually that his life-story and the reasons for his unhappiness emerge.

By profession, Chisholm is a soldier with a dogged patriotism to a country which sustains him in his various personal trials. Chief cause of his misery at the novel's opening is his pain and demoralising shame at his brother's execution for cowardice on the field of battle. This fretting, despite his own acquisition of a Military Cross, brings him to the verge of nervous collapse, undermining his self-confidence to the extent that, entrusted with military mission to the Faeroes, he unloads his responsibilities onto a naval officer, the ultra-self-confident Dick Silver:

> [...] so immediate, so enveloping, was the feeling I had of his strength and competence that I was already prepared, I suppose, to accept him as my leader. (**C** p. 43, **B** p. 44)

This deference to Silver's decisive personality continues when they encounter the traitor Mungo Wishart and Silver's suspicions of his treason are proved correct. With Wishart's suicide, Chisholm is overcome with guilt at what he feels is his complicity in the death of the father of two innocent children, Olaf and Gudrun, a circumstance which he tells us 'lay on my mind like a charge of murder.' (**C** p. 147, **B** p. 157) The weight of his 'guilt' (together with his family 'shame') is such that he 'hoped to see [himself] killed' (**C** p. 148, **B** p. 158) when he is subsequently posted to North Africa.

Here and later in Italy, Chisholm's death wish is exorcised when he is forced to confront death at first hand. Three incidents shock him out of his self-recriminations: in North Africa an unknown 'squaddie' saves the life of Chisholm and a colleague but dies himself in the act; in Italy, his brother's commanding officer (and executioner), much hated by Chisholm, astonishes Tony by giving his life to save his troops and, finally, Tony himself is shocked into parallel bravery when he rushes to the rescue of soldiers under attack. The discovery of this strength of compassion, previously unrecognised in himself, banishes much of his earlier personal disengagement with life:

> It was pity expanding to indignation – to an indignant refusal to allow such pain to cry for help, unanswered – that had broken down the persistent coldness of my temper, the caution of my spirit [...] (**C** p. 170, **B** p. 180)

In reacting in this warm-blooded, spontaneous way to the plight of others rather than isolating himself in cold introspection, as he had been doing, he finds to his delight:

> [...] but for the trifling cost of a broken leg I had made myself whole. (**C** p. 170, **B** p. 181)

This wholeness, however, is interrupted when, in the Korean war, he has to cope with both the death of Olaf Wishart and the amputation of his own left arm. Grief and physical mutilation see Chisholm plunging back to another low point in his morale. Interestingly, it is at this point that Silver resurfaces in the novel with a tempting offer of a new life in the Far East. Although appearing weakened by events, Chisholm's loyalty to elements in his background (albeit ones he finds difficult to define), gives him the strength to resist the once influential Silver.

Ultimately it is his calling as a soldier that sees him through this difficult period, overriding as it does any personal ambition like that of Silver. It is this army career, far from limiting his life, which ultimately gives it a new affirmation of purpose in the post-Korean world. He finds himself a soldier of NATO in Versailles and:

> It was, from the beginning, an exhilarating feeling [...]
> (**C** p. 232, **B** p. 246)

This broader concept of loyalty – international rather than narrowly national – sees a lifting of the spirits of a man who has observed only too closely the dangers and miseries wrought by narrow, nationalistic causes espoused by men like Wishart and the politicians who directed the wars Chisholm and men like him have just survived.

This new optimism and self-confidence is liberating to Chisholm the man as well as Chisholm the soldier, for it is only now that he can find emotional as well as professional fulfilment. Finally, he can let go the corrosive memories of guilt and betrayal, personal and collective, which have clouded much of his adult life as he contemplates his new life with Gudrun.

Lieutenant Dick Silver

> He was a man of my own age, or a little more, with a narrow, finely moulded head and thick dark hair [...] His arms and body were well muscled, his hands and feet long and thin; as if bone were reaching out for eloquence. But more impressive than his physical appearance was his whole manner and demeanour of natural assurance [...] (**C** p. 42, **B** p. 44)

Silver is a lieutenant in the Naval Volunteer Reserve with the 'natural confidence of one who had never dreamt that his word could be disputed' (**C** p. 46, **B** p. 48) and captain of the trawler which takes Chisholm to the Faeroes. Apart from playing a key role in the unmasking of Mungo Wishart, Silver's function in the novel is that of a foil to the character of Chisholm. With his 'demeanour of natural assurance' he is everything that Tony feels he is not. Tony, undergoing as he is a total collapse of self-confidence after his interview with Pelly, instantly feels overshadowed by Silver's commanding personality and tells us he was 'already prepared [...] to accept him as my leader' (**C** p. 43, **B** p. 44) Chisholm defers totally to his assured judgment in dealing with Torur and

Bomlo and later with Mungo Wishart. Silver belongs confidently in the world of certainties, a fact suggested by his passion for mathematics. In his openness to the world of books, art and ballet he contrasts sharply with Chisholm, totally turned in as he is on his own personal woes and problems. As Tony puts it:

> [...] he seemed so wholly the master of his own world [...]
> (C p. 46, B p. 48)

After his role in unmasking Wishart, Silver largely disappears from the novel. He makes one brief appearance in Chapter 11 where Chisholm notes a growing cynicism in him with regard to the war, feeling let down by what he feels is Britain's lack of a cause. For him, fighting for survival is not enough. He reappears shortly after the death of Olaf Wishart and the amputation of Tony's left arm. Here again his role appears to be to point up differences between himself and Chisholm. He comes to visit the hospitalised Tony in Singapore. Both men are now much changed, as is the dynamic of their interdependence. Where once Chisholm needed Silver, their roles are reversed. Silver, now a rich man, is anxious to obtain Tony's organisational skills to help run his successful Far Eastern shipping company:

> [...] he needed me now – and yet, though his friendship pleased and flattered me, I had little difficulty in refusing it [...] (C p. 205, B p. 217–18)

While Silver, disillusioned by the war, has abandoned his life in Britain for the comfortable life of the rich exile, Tony realises he needs a life of service to others for real personal happiness.

While war has seen Tony grow in spiritual stature, Silver has been somewhat diminished by it:

> His air of dash and daring was carried now, as it seemed, on a rather tired habit of dash and daring; not, as before, on a constantly renewing impulse. (C p. 201, B p. 213)

No longer in awe of Silver as once he was, Chisholm's first comment is on the superficial theatricality of Silver's appearance:

> "You look," I said, "like a character out of Conrad." – And immediately I was sorry for my perception [...]
> (**C** p. 200, **B** p. 212)

Once, he would have been only too happy to fall in with any of Silver's suggestions, but now he remains loyal to his creed of service to others, rather than to Silver's new rather self-serving principles. Silver is no longer the object of Tony's hero worship. Silver, who despite his financial success and easy life, has given up reading and fails to understand Tony's spontaneous heroism. (**C** p. 202, **B** p. 213) While war has seen a flowering of Chisholm's personality, Silver's has turned inwards on itself; now he is a man engaged entirely with personal gratification rather than exploring the world of books and ideas as once he did:

> "Stay here with me, Tony. Marry a Chinese girl, make money, and enjoy yourself. And to hell with causes."
> (**C** p. 207, **B** p. 219)

Now, the course of his war has taught Tony only too well the toll which the dedication to causes brings to nations and individuals; but he is also wary of the other extreme: the espousing of personal gratification which is Silver's response to war. Silver's reaction is perhaps understandable but its self-serving nature helps throw into sharper relief the more public-spirited, generous-hearted nature of Chisholm's final life choice.

Mungo Wishart

Wishart is the laird of Weddergarth, owner of several thousand acres of land, and father of Olaf and Gudrun, the girl who eventually becomes Tony Chisholm's wife. Silver informs Chisholm that:

He has a local reputation for eccentricity, bad temper, and a solitary habit. (C p. 83, B p. 87)

This disagreeability of character is borne out when Chisholm meets him, when forced by sudden illness to take refuge at Weddergarth:

> There was indeed something in his features reminiscent of the righteous arrogance, the intolerant assurance of their own rectitude, that marked, and gave distinction to, so many Victorian soldiers and the pro-consuls of our eastern empire. (C p. 118, B p. 126)

A former consular official in the Near East, he harbours a loathing for Lloyd George in particular and his country in general for what he sees as its duplicitous treatment of the tribes of Armenia, Azerbaijan and Georgia. He harbours a similar contempt for Britain's treatment of Ireland and of Roger Casement, the man shot by Britain as a spy. Chisholm's reading of Wishart's history of his family reveals that Mungo also feels outrage at his own family's treacherous treatment of Old Dandy Pitcairn. He is a deeply unhappy man, one seething with anger, with Chisholm noting that he had 'the temper of a fanatic' and that 'there was madness in him'. (C p. 123, B p. 131)

But Chisholm also noted:

> [...] while his interminable harangue went on and on, and filled the world with chicanery, lies and people betrayed, I could recognise in him a perverted goodness, and in his face see a wild nobility. (C p. 123, B p. 131)

This sense of 'people betrayed' has led him to meet betrayal with betrayal, by involving himself in shady dealings with the infamous Nazi puppet Quisling, claiming that Britain could only be saved by some eccentric scheme of alliance between Northern countries. In his harangue he tells Chisholm:

The last dregs of Norse blood had run out, and there was no
hope for Britain unless its heart could be replenished.
(C p. 125, B p. 133)

How this blood is to be replenished is never made clear to us or to Chisholm, but when his Nazi connections are detected by Silver, Wishart's reaction is swift: he commits suicide, clearly fearing that his treachery in time of war will lead to him being shot as a traitor.

But there is, too, clearly 'a wild nobility' in him as his quotation from Yeats' poem 'The Curse of Cromwell' tends to suggest. It seems he did once have an idealistic belief in Britain, but over the years, this has been replaced by a disenchanted hatred, one nurtured by his sense of betrayal:

I came upon a great house in the middle of the night,
Its open lighted doorway and its windows all alight,
And all my friends were there and made me welcome too;
But I woke in an old ruin that the winds howled through.
(C p.121, B p. 129)

Britain's present state, as the 'great house' fallen on hard times, has turned sour his former vision of it, resulting in his treachery towards what he sees as the 'old ruin'.

His reaction to what he sees as betrayal is in marked contrast to that of Chisholm who is no stranger either to a sense of family betrayal or a feeling that he is fighting for a country that is much reduced from what once it was:

The Britain to which I was born was in every way shabbier
and poorer – materially, spiritually, in political influence –
than the Britain my parents had known [...]
(C p. 3, B p. 4)

But his response is very different from that of Wishart. The methodical, unimaginative Quartermaster quietly carries on serving his country; the disillusioned, flamboyant idealist betrays it – and dies by his own hand. For him there can be none of the feeling of 'wholeness' which is the reward which awaits Chisholm after his career of war service.

Both men have suffered from the corrosive power of memory: remembered wrongs poison both lives. It is Wishart, however, who indirectly furnishes Chisholm with an idea that allows him to exorcise eventually this corrosive power. Contradicting an idea in Wordsworth's 'Intimations of Immortality', Wishart insists in his family history that:

> "Memory is the curse of man, the curse of nations. No man who remembers, no country that can never forget, has ever lived happily or ever will." (**C** pp. 175–76, **B** p. 186)

Yet Wishart, ironically, cannot translate this belief into his own life. Unlike Chisholm, he never learns how to let go of the past and suicide seems a welcome escape from his miserable existence.

BIBLIOGRAPHY

Novels
White-Maa's Saga (1929)
Poet's Pub (1929)
Juan in America (1931)
The Men of Ness (1932)
Magnus Merriman (1934)
Ripeness is All (1935)
The Sailor's Holiday (1937)
Juan in China (1937)
The Impregnable Women (1938)
Judas (1939)
Private Angelo (1946)
A Spell for Old Bones (1949)
Mr Byculla (1950)
Laxdale Hall (1951)
The House of Gair (1953)
The Faithful Ally (1954)
The Dark of Summer (1956)
Position at Noon (1958)
The Merry Muse (1959)
Roll of Honour (1961)
Husband of Delilah (1962)
A Man Over Forty (1963)
A Terrible Freedom (1966)

Autobiographies
The Man On My Back (1941)
A Year of Space (1953)
Fanfare for a Tin Hat (1970)

Further Reading
Hall, Simon W.: *The History of Orkney Literature*, Edinburgh: Birlinn, 2010
Massie, Allan: "The Linklater Lecture", *Aberdeen University Newsletter*: Aberdeen, July, 1999
Murray, Isobel: *Scottish Novels of the Second World War*, Edinburgh: WP Books, 2011
Parnell, Michael: *Eric Linklater: a Critical Biography*, London: John Murray, 1984

Lightning Source UK Ltd.
Milton Keynes UK
UKOW05f1849061215

264166UK00001B/25/P